Direct Mail Pal—Canada

Direct Mail Pal—Canada

A Direct Mail Production Handbook Serving the Informational Needs of the Canadian Direct Mail Industry

By

T.J. Tedesco

John Leonard

David Engel

PIA/GATF Press

Pittsburgh

PIA/GATF*Press* books are widely used by companies, associations, and schools for training, marketing, and resale. Quantity discounts are available by contacting PIA/GATF Order Department at the number below.

PIA/GATF*Press*
Printing Industries of America/
   Graphic Arts Technical Foundation
200 Deer Run Road
Sewickley, PA 15143-2600
Phone: 412/741-6860
Fax: 412/741-2311
Email: AWoodall@piagatf.org
Internet: www.gain.net

Orders to:
Online: www.gain.net
PIA/GATF Orders
200 Deer Run Road
Sewickley, PA 15143
Phone (U.S. and Canada):
  866/855-4283
Phone (all other countries):
  301/393-8624
Fax: 301/393-2555

Contents

Section 3—Direct Mail Production

Appendices

Glossaries

Index

About the Authors

This book is dedicated to the authors' children.

May they always know they are first in their Dads' hearts.

Daniel Engel
Paul Engel
Tina Engel
Chloe Leonard
Sydney Leonard
Luke Tedesco
Sofia Tedesco

Preface

Who should read this book? The target audience for *Direct Mail Pal—Canada* can be divided into two main categories:

1. *Printing and direct mail customer service and sales professionals, estimators, production managers, and lettershop and bindery employees*

Growth-oriented printing and direct mail companies recognize that the training process never stops. This comprehensive book will be both informational and accessible to mid- and entry-level direct mail and printing professionals. Basic direct mail knowledge is an under-represented skill set in the graphic arts industry and those with a good command of these processes will do their jobs better. Careful study of this book will help readers advance their careers.

2. *Marketers, agency employees, and graphic designers*

Many marketers and graphic designers have misconceptions of what is possible, or what is cost-effective when planning direct mail programs. These misconceptions hamper their ability to serve their clients and limits their professional growth. Marketers and designers will appreciate down-to-earth descriptions of direct mail processes without being overly technical.

Acknowledgments

This book wouldn't have been possible without contributions from some extraordinary people and their organizations.

Special thanks go to **Ken Boone** and **Terry Woods** who:
- Were the founders of Direct Marketing Associates
- Were important team leaders within Harte Hanks, Inc.
- Are well recognized visionaries of the direct mail industry. Their contributions will have a long lasting impact.

The authors would like to thank the following people for multiple significant contributions scattered throughout various parts of this book:
- **Mark Beard,** president, Finishbinders, Inc.
- **David Clossey,** partner, Grow Sales, Inc.
- **Dave Frantz,** president, Direct Concepts
- **Scott MacMurchy,** direct mail specialist, Relizon
- **Jack Rickard,** president, Rickard Bindery
- **Frank Shear,** president, Seaboard Bindery
- **Art Simpson,** president, EU Services
- **Adam Van Wye,** vice president, Mailing Lists, Inc.

In addition, appreciation needs to be extended to several direct mail and printing industry editors for all their guidance, patience, and support throughout the years. They are:
- **Scott Hovanyetz,** associate editor, and **Tad Clark,** editor of *DM News*
- **David Lindsay,** editor-in-chief of various Cygnus Business Media, Inc. publications
- **Mark Michelson,** editor-in-chief of *Printing Impressions*
- **Katherine O'Brien,** editorial director of *American Printer*
- **Ray Roth,** editor-in-chief, and **Mary Ellin Innes,** president of Innes Publishing Co.
- **Nancy Scott,** editor of *Advents*
- **Roger Ynostroza,** former editor-in-chief of *Graphic Arts Monthly*

Other important contributions were made by Jeff Alt,
Marty Anson, Brian Bock, Steve Bock, Jerry Bridges,
Rick Carletti, Kevin Coyne, Fred Daubert, David Dunnett,
Chris Eckhart, Jim Egan, Jim Feldman, Barry Franklin,
John Goche, John Helline, Brian Hills, Kurt Hoffman,
Tony Hoholik, Bob Janes, Harold Jones, Gary Junge,
Russ Haines, Sue Hein, Michael Keene, Jeff Klein,
Adam Lerner, John Mackey, Bill Maguire, Gary Markovits,
Robert Mason, Gary McCants, Bob Miller, Peter Pape,
Pete Perlo, Kevin Rickard, Carlos Rodriguez, Bruce Sanderson,
Mark Sanderson, Tom Schultz, Bill Seidl, Frank Shear,
Harold Shear, Jim Shear, Sylvia Taylor, Bob Tier, Mike Welsch,
and Kathi Young.

Foreword

Why was this book written? In 2002, the first edition of the
Direct Mail Pal (DMP) was published. The intention was to
combine direct mail production from both a U.S. and
Canadian vantage point. However, the difference between
the two countries' postal systems makes a Canadian-only
version necessary. The authors apologize for the delay, but
we hope that you find the wait worth it.

Direct Mail Pal—Canada will take readers through a comprehensive exploration of the world of direct mail from the
Canadian perspective. Against the backdrop of more promotional options than ever before, we will present the ongoing
benefits of direct mail in a positive, but realistic light.

Direct Mail Pal—Canada is comprised of four main sections:
- **Direct Mail Today**—Common direct mail concepts and
  products
- **Direct Mail Pre-Production**—Project planning, layouts, and
  front-end data concepts
- **Direct Mail Production**—Data management, imaging, lettershop, and bindery operations
- **Appendices**—Practical direct mail nuts and bolts information
  for everyday use

In the first section, we'll establish that effective marketing
depends on using the best available promotional tools to
influence buying behavior. None of the big four promotional
categories —direct sales, airwave media, direct mail/printing,
and e-commerce/Internet—are going to disappear anytime
soon. Media convergence is a good thing, even for those in
the direct mail industry. As many dot-com companies have
discovered, the inherent promotional weakness of the e-world
means that the demand for promotional printed materials
such as direct mail will increase for the foreseeable future.
This section will also cover some important general business

concepts including account management, communication, and quality assurance.

In sections two and three, we'll get to the heart of direct mail planning, production, and analysis. The topics discussed will be pertinent for most entry- and mid-level professionals.

Unlike many other books, the appendices deserve careful review. This is where you can find useful nuts and bolts operating tips, procedures, and management forms. Put this section to work for your organization.

Introduction

In this age of staggering media choices and rapidly evolving digital marketing tools, the book you hold in your hands is more relevant than ever. Direct mail still reigns supreme for its ability to target, qualify, convince, and convert prospects into valuable long-term customers. And mail is an outstanding tool for keeping those customers loyal and profitable.

I have been a great proponent of direct mail since the late 1970s, but I have also heartily embraced online marketing since the late 1980s. I am quite excited about the promise that the new technologies have delivered to our industry. However, as much as I have taken significant advantage of the new media tools and opportunities, I continue to rely on direct mail to produce results in ways that the new media still cannot match.

Time and time again, marketers have quantifiably proven that direct mail has the power to deliver highly qualified customers—customers who afford you greater revenue, renew better, contribute more, and deliver significantly greater lifetime value to the bottom line.

In all fairness, no single media choice fills every targeting or marketing solution. But direct mail is often a brilliant choice as an integrated component of campaigns that involve hand-raising and conversion of individual buyers. And it is an even more masterful choice for leveraging the greatest return from those existing pools of customers.

I sometimes shake my head in disbelief when marketers unfamiliar with our business insist that direct mail is no longer viable due to the high cost per contact. Nonsense! Direct mail can produce some of the best revenue streams from a pool of customers.

It addition to the high-value customers that it creates, direct mail's tactile nature still reassures recipients and helps them find value and confidence in it. This comfort of the physical printed piece has proven to be a great defense against the assault from spam, phishing, pharming, or whichever additional online schemes will no doubt evolve after this book goes to print.

But there is a catch. In order for you to take advantage of direct mail's benefits, you must not only be a savvy marketer, but you must have flawless execution in the finished product. That's what this book is all about—ensuring that you get the greatest returns from your mailing by guaranteeing what you intended to produce actually gets produced, and ensuring who you intended to target actually receives the most relevant message in the most efficient manner.

This book will save you from making costly errors in your planning and execution. More important, it will help you harness mail to its fullest potential.

Who will benefit from this book? Any production person who is tasked with getting a piece into the mail should always have this book close at hand. Even production veterans will find a wealth of new insights into their own approaches. As for the more junior production people, I honestly don't know how they can survive and contribute fully without the information and guidance contained in this text.

I would suggest that this book should also be required reading for brand managers, advertising agency account executives, business owners, or anyone who might ever remotely find a role for direct mail as part of their marketing mix. Strategic marketers and tactical executors alike will be excited by the new possibilities this book uncovers.

Equally as important, this text will be invaluable to any creative person who has to write or design an effective piece for the mail. Their creative juices can only be sparked by having a better understanding of what is possible and where the production process can take their ideas. I've yet to see a writer who doesn't light up when given the chance to take advantage of expanded personalization opportunities. It is equally thrilling to see a designer escape from the confines of a traditional mail package, yet still do it economically and effectively.

Personally, I am convinced this book should be required reading for anyone planning, assigning, creating, critiquing, or running any business that currently produces or might benefit from direct mail.

I congratulate you on adding the *Direct Mail Pal* to your marketing and production library. This book will save you time. It will save you money. It will help you produce more efficient and effective direct mail pieces. It will be an invaluable reference for years to come, as it will continue to be for me.

Daniel G. Wiest
President, Wiest & Associates Inc.—The Customer Acquisition and Retention Company™
www.wiest.ca

———

Past Chair, Canadian Marketing Association Annual Convention and Trade Show

Past Chair, Canadian Marketing Association Annual Digital Marketing Conference

Executive Member, CMA e-Marketing Council

Instructor: CMA Direct Marketing Certification Program

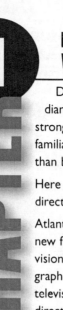

Direct Mail: A Compelling Way to Spread Your Word

Does direct mail work? Just a quick look into any Canadian mailbox on any normal business day will give you a strong indication. One of the authors remembers his father's familiar lament: "I wish I'd get something in the mail other than bills." Apparently, he got his wish.

Here are some examples that demonstrate the power of direct mail.

Atlantic Blue Cross Care ran a campaign to boost sales of a new flexible care product. The campaign included both a television advertisement and a direct mail campaign to demographically selected postal codes in Atlantic Canada. While television yielded 12% of the campaign's response volume, the direct mail piece was responsible for a far larger percentage: *nearly half of all responses!* Even more impressive is that the acquisition cost of new customers from the television ads was nearly twice that of direct mail.

The Royal Canadian Mint found success in direct mail as well. By mailing catalogs to active buyers, they achieved a 10% increase in revenue as well as a 260% increase in order size.

The phenomenal success of *How to Win Friends and Influence People* by Dale Carnegie was in part due to a direct mail piece that directly accounted for a million books being sold in three years.

When subscription rates need to be boosted, where do high-profile magazines like *Athletics*, *Profit*, and *Maclean's* turn? Direct mail once again.

How about companies like Air France, Apple Computer, Blockbuster Video, Colgate-Palmolive, Sony, the U.S. Army, and Nintendo? They all rely on direct mail for one reason: it works.

According to Canada Post Corporation (CPC), Canadians spend more than $12 billion annually on direct response mail with an estimated annual growth of 10%. CPC operating revenues from Unaddressed and Addressed Admail™ reached $786 million, an increase of 6.4% between 2004 and 2005.

Why does this seemingly old-fashioned method of contacting customers and prospects have such an attractive future? Unlike broadcast and print advertising media that does not elicit a direct response, direct mail is accountable. Every cent involved in producing a direct mail campaign is easily tallied and each response can be tracked. Future decisions can be made based on past results. Combining today's abundant wealth of consumer data with sophisticated imaging technology means that true one-to-one direct response marketing is a reality.

It's a testament to our industry when an advertising legend such as David Olgivy, founder of the high-profile advertising agency Olgivy & Mather, claims that direct mail was his first love and secret weapon.

> I have been a voice crying in the wilderness, trying to persuade the advertising establishment to take direct mail more seriously and to stop treating its practitioners as non-commissioned officers. It was my secret weapon in the avalanche of new business acquisitions that made Olgivy & Mather an instant success. (David Olgivy, 1983)

PAL POINT... No matter your involvement in the advertising and promotional industries, do right by your customers by being a strong direct mail advocate. Make sound business decisions by correctly assessing your promotional and informational needs, choosing the right direct mail options, and then evaluating your results. In short, learn your craft well so you can be a valuable resource to your company and customers.

A Brief History of Direct Mail

In some respects, mailing is an extension of the graphic arts industry. Like printers and trade binderies, direct mailing services companies enhance the value of paper by changing its form. The direct mail industry is constantly evolving, and today it is vastly different than it was as recently as twenty years ago.

Let's start by saying that direct mail marketing is the means of targeting individuals with the highest propensity to respond to a marketing or other promotional message. Every production issue theoretically is in pursuit of achieving this objective. Once established, we are free to move on to various production issues.

Top-quality prepress, printing, binding, and finishing services do not make a bit of difference unless the final printed product gets into the hands of the target audience. Today, there is still no better way to quickly deliver large quantities of printed products than direct mail. To better manage the direct mail process, it is useful to understand how our seemingly complicated mailing environment came to be.

Direct Mail Processing

In the late 1960s the computer found its way into list maintenance. At this point, the direct mail industry rapidly changed from metal plate addressing, to data card addressing, to computerized label generation. With computers, maintaining mailing files became significantly easier, and record "selection" (targeted mailings) became feasible. Although most databases were developed and maintained by individual companies, the end product was generally four-up Cheshire labels printed in Postal Code order.

Canada Post Corporation (CPC) attempted postal cost reduction by encouraging large volume mailers to prepare their mailings in a fashion that would minimize postal handling. CPC offers a discount for any form of presorted mail, which reduces postage costs for mail prepared by individual carrier route. By giving mail bundles directly to mail carriers, CPC eliminates a number of sorting steps, and costs go down. Appending letter carrier route information to data files while simultaneously pursuing the postal discount qualification process caused many mailers to abandon homegrown software in favor of standard presort programs.

Throughout much of 1980s, mail presorting was primarily done on mainframe computers with expensive software. In the 1990s, this software became widely available on PCs and a large number of individual users became capable of preparing their own mailing files. The output of these presorting programs slowly changed from Cheshire labels to an electronic medium capable of driving high-speed inkjet and laser printers.

Mail Preparation

Mail preparation equipment has evolved from slow simple machines requiring a lot of workers to fast, automated, single-operator ones. Today, high-speed imaging devices have largely replaced Cheshire labels. While there are many imaging techniques available, the direct mail industry is dominated by laser and inkjet printing. Customers seeking high quality and large image areas generally prefer laser printing. If personalization is required on only a small portion of the printed product (i.e., name and address), inkjet printing is more attractive.

Recently, great strides have been made toward bridging the quality gap between inkjet and laser printing. Today, there are inkjet units that not only produce images as large as laser printer output (with the same font selection), but also do so faster and cheaper. The resolution standard for inkjet printing is now 300×300 dpi while laser printing is 600 dpi or even higher. After imaging, more online or offline post press processes can be done or the job can directly enter the mail stream. Generally, laser printed forms are personalized box-to-box or roll-to-roll, then converted, folded, and glue-sealed, tab-sealed, or inserted into an envelope. A lot of time and money can be saved when inkjet imaging is done inline with other paper conversion processes.

The final step is to correctly package the mail to maximize postal discounts. Mailbags, like Cheshire labels, are all but dead. Postal Trays called "lettertainers" and their larger siblings, usually referred to as "tubs," are now the norm for presorted mail and do a much better job at protecting the mail given their hard plastic construction.

PAL POINT... Direct mail has changed a lot. Over the years, the emphasis has drifted from mechanical efficiency to electronic wizardry. In addition, keeping abreast of the changing postal climate is more important now than ever. Investing the time to find the right mailing partner and develop a good working relationship with your postal representative will significantly benefit you...and likely save you a lot of money.

Convergence: Direct Mail, Electronic, Print, and Airwave Media

Today, many people consider time as their most valuable asset. Direct mail is a uniquely effective way to reach people because it allows consumers to gather information about goods, services, or almost anything else whenever and wherever they want. Good information is required to make educated buying decisions. To that end, direct mail is an invaluable asset. We're going to take a step back for a moment and consider all print media, including direct mail for this chapter.

Are you concerned about the e-commerce wave? Can you remember a time when the graphic arts and advertising industries didn't feel "threatened" by one new technology or another? First, it was the telephone, then radio, TV, and the "paperless society." Sure, each development affected business, but as long as those in the direct mail industry caught the wave, we were fine. Smart direct marketers aren't scared of e-commerce, instead they are just dusting off their surfboards.

There is sustainable growth in some direct mail markets, and our challenge is to position our own companies by making the right strategic choices. Smart marketers will take advantage of the best promotional tools available to them and select a mix of marketing vehicles that achieves their business goals. E-commerce will have a vital role to play—and so will print and its subset, direct mail.

A large percentage of commercially printed matter attempts to separate customers from their discretionary dollars. Until recently, marketers had three primary categories of promotional activities within which to engage:
• Sales—In person, telephone, or email
• Airwaves—Radio or television
• Print—Direct mail, advertising, billboards, etc.

Now, they have one more:

• E-commerce—Transactions over the Internet

Throw out the hype. As exciting as e-commerce is, it really is just another category of promotional tool in a savvy marketer's arsenal. Each category has pros and cons.

The Big Four

Sales. Sales activity is very personal and very effective. However, a sales force is an expensive proposition and is inappropriate for many types of products and services.

Airwaves. TV and radio reach a lot of people at a relatively low cost per impression. However, the Achilles Heel of air-wave media is that the pitch gets to the consumer on the advertiser's schedule, not the consumer's. This means that both TV and radio are poorly suited for direct response because most people can't remember phone numbers, store locations and website addresses unless they happen to have a writing or recording instrument handy. Viewers and listeners will get a basic idea about what is being pitched, but taking action is difficult. Moreover, channel surfing during commercials seems to be on the rise.

Printing and Direct Mail. Print is convenient. One of the major benefits of this category is that people can view promotional materials on their own schedule, not the advertisers'. Then, if they choose to take action, they can bring the printed piece with them for reference purposes while making telephone calls or accessing websites. Yes, some forms of print behave more like airwave media (i.e., billboards and signage), but print in general and direct mail in specific is easily stored and highly portable.

The Internet. The Internet offers improvement over both print and airwave marketing in two significant ways. First, it performs exceptionally well for executing simple transactions in a "point and click" environment. Second, it is a low-cost way to provide lots of information to the marketplace and keep it current. However, as a promotional medium, the Internet is still relatively weak. Soliciting to "opt-in" lists is for the meantime OK, but as people get more and more fed up with email and banner advertising overload, click-through rates will continue to plunge. On the other hand, the recent popularity of paid advertising searches (i.e., Google™, Yahoo!™ or others) is likely to increase the value of commercial time spent on the Internet.

Other Factors

There are other topics to consider. First, direct mail pieces can be almost any size, giving this media an unencumbered field of vision. Although electronic pages can be unlimited in size too, their practical viewing area is limited by the size of the viewer's computer monitor. Side-by-side product comparisons from different companies are easy to do if the medium is print—just spread out competing catalogs and brochures on a large flat surface. Comparison-shopping on the web is possible, but it requires toggling prowess and effective management of limited viewing space.

Also, current pixel technology means that image reproduction on many computer monitors is of lesser quality than print. For example, consider how people buy furniture. Stores, catalogs, and websites are three popular ways. As in many businesses, maintaining low return rates is critically important. Return rates are lowest when customers' expectations are met. When you buy furniture off a store floor, you're pretty sure about the quality you're going to get. When you order from an image, whether it be digital or printed, the product better match your expectations or you might return it. In order to attract business, furniture dotcoms offer extremely liberal return policies to convince their target audiences to try their services. This can be a dangerous way of doing business—as Living.com discovered when its return rate exceeded 40%, causing it to go out of business. The bottom line is that images must accurately depict the product, and print is still best at doing this.

What Are Smart Marketers Doing?

According to a widely accepted business school marketing model, marketers should lead their target audiences through the four AIDA steps—awareness, interest, desire, and action. A reasonable strategy is to first choose shotgun-style air-wave and print (magazines, newspapers, billboards, etc.) media to garner market awareness. Next, use rifle vehicles like targeted direct mail and tele-prospecting to generate buying interest. Then, apply direct sales principles to create desire. And finally, use interactive media, like the Internet, call centers, or direct-response print to get customers to take action (buy).

As always, effective marketing relies on using the best available tools to influence buying behavior. None of the big four promotional categories is going to disappear anytime soon. Media convergence is a good thing, even for those of us with our livelihoods tied to the direct mail industry. As information continues to migrate from print to the Internet, manuals and catalogs will become thinner and less important. However, the technological advantages of the e-world form the

Slider self-mailer, used in conjunction with other media. (Courtesy Innovative Graphics)

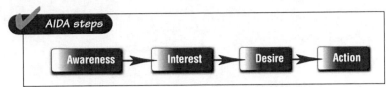

basis of its inherent promotional weakness. Without a proven promotional medium like direct mail to drive traffic to websites, even great information stands a good chance of remaining undescovered.

PAL POINT... In 1939, *New York Times* predicted that the automatic typewriter was going to make the pen and pencil obsolete. This didn't happen. Sure, the typewriter forced these industries to sharpen their strategies, but they thrived for six more decades and will continue to do so. Now some traditional manufacturers, like the A.T. Cross Pen Company for instance, are making forays into the digital arena with high-tech electronic products. Instead of feeling threatened, let's wish them well.

An Overview of CPC Mail Classifications and Rates

CPC offers various rates for its service of delivering the mail. This rate structure is dependent upon two factors:

1. **Delivery speed and quality.** CPC is betting that customers will pay a premium for quicker and more reliable mail flow.

2. **Work sharing.** CPC is willing to offer postal discounts if the customer shares in the preparation of their mail. The better prepared your mail, the less CPC has to handle it. This reduces CPC processing costs and mailers that undertake these efforts are offered a lower rate structure.

Service

Most mail into CPC's mail stream is either entered as Lettermail or Addressed Admail™. There are other classes of mail such as Unaddressed Admail, Dimensional Admail™, and Publications Mail (a classification for magazines, newsletters, and newspapers). Lettermail is a very broad category, and is the one with which most Canadians are familiar. Common usages include personal letters of correspondence, bill payment, typical business letters, and so forth. Since studies show that promotional materials with Lettermail postage enjoys a high rate of being opened, some companies will use Lettermail on large volume promotional mailings, but this is very expensive.

Addressed Admail is a way to significantly reduce your postal costs, however you may not mail individual pieces of Admail to your Aunt Edna because there are minimum-piece requirements. Like many businesses, CPC is willing to reduce the fees they charge if their customers give them large enough orders and make preparation easier than usual. Remember the work sharing concept?

The main differences between Lettermail and Addressed Admail are three-fold: (1) delivery speed, (2) return to sender services, and (3) cost. In most cases, Lettermail will get to the designated recipients days faster and if undeliverable, will be returned to the sender. Conversely, undeliverable Addressed Admail will not be returned without adding a premium price to each piece. Additionally, address correction services will about double your postal costs. Lettermail senders pay a substantial premium over Addressed Admail, about one third more on average, and higher in many circumstances. If you intend on sending many mailings to the same list, it might pay to make your first mailing Lettermail or Addressed Admail with the endorsements for extra costs to correct or remove all returns, and then send the rest of your mailings out via standard Addressed Admail.

Advertising by Mail—Do You Qualify?

To determine whether a mail piece is promotional, ask the question, "What is the intent of the piece?" If the intent is to motivate an individual to buy or acquire a product or service, or to contribute to or support a cause, it is promotional and therefore acceptable as Addressed Admail.

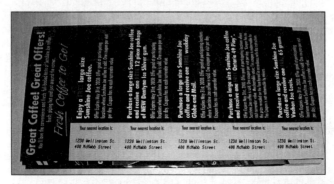

Unaddressed program localized by using variable inkjet technology. (Courtesy SMR•Tytrek)

If you're looking for a very inexpensive pricing structure, Unaddressed Admail may be for you. However, in exchange for rock-bottom prices, there are some significant trade-offs: no individual addresses, no returns, and no corrections. This form of mail is close to shotgun advertising. The only method of targeting recipients is via postal code and letter carrier walk.

Addressed Admail requires a "Statement of Accuracy," discussed later in this book. In every instance, cost considerations have to be weighed with the delivery requirements.

Work Sharing

Whether you are mailing Lettermail, Addressed, or Un-addressed Admail, CPC will give you discounts on mass mailings if you perform the following services yourself:

1. **Put the mail in proper order.** This is known as presorting the mail, and it requires using Postal Codes and other postal identification codes (i.e., appended letter carrier walk number) to properly sequence the mail. CPC-approved commercial software programs perform this service for high-volume mailers. This category of software also standardizes addresses, which is a CPC requirement. Although no specific discount is given for this function, a surcharge applies if this process is not performed.

2. **Mail piece design.** CPC allows discounted rates if your mail piece conforms to postal standards. In general, you're rewarded for small and light designs. Why? Simply because more pieces of smaller and light mail can be transported by the same resources. As long as your mail isn't too small and light for postal sorting machinery, it is only fair that you receive some of CPC's cost savings. The most typical classifications of mail are "Short," "Long," and "Oversize." Short and Long cannot exceed

245×156×5 mm (9.65×6.14×0.02 in.). And Oversize
cannot exceed 380×270×20 mm (14.97×10.63×0.79 in.).

Please note that Addressed Admail customers are required
to run their data through a CPC-approved address accuracy
program, even though no discount is offered. A copy of this
file must be made available upon request and be 95% accurate
or higher to avoid postal cost penalties.

PAL POINT... The concept of work sharing is very important for high-volume mailers. As we discuss at length in the
production sections of this book, tremendous savings are available to mailers that undertake some mail preparation tasks
themselves. Work sharing is truly a win-win-win proposition—
for the client, the mail services company, and CPC.

Postal Rate Changes: A Fact of Life

The three universals of life used to be death, taxes, and laundry. Now add a fourth: postal rate changes—usually increases of course! The bad news is that some short-sighted direct mailers may run scared during rate hikes and temporarily reduce the frequency and size of their direct mail programs.

On the other hand, the good news about rate hikes is three-fold. First, when defecting postal customers discover that their marketing results are suffering, they will come roaring back. Second, postal rate turbulence means there is a greater need for direct marketers—such as those reading this book—to provide leadership to help their customers navigate through direct mail's increasingly choppy waters. Third, marketers will be forced to target more efficiently and effectively. While not always popular, in the long run, this trend will be good for the direct response industry. It is important for Canadian legislators to remember that for every percentage of postal rate increase, a corresponding decrease in direct mail volume will occur or at least has in the past.

Direct mail pros constantly remain abreast of all postal rate laws and changes. Those with knowledge are in control. If you can position yourself at your company and in your business community as a postal knowledge leader, those with large scale of mailings and the budgets will value you for having accurate information at your fingertips. Companies are less likely to halt or reduce mailing campaigns when they have adequate knowledge of rate changes because it allows them time to get budgetary approvals as necessary. Be certain that these changes are properly communicated internally. The last place you want a rate surprise is at the CPC counter. At this point, it is very hard to go back to your client and inform them that you miscalculated their postal costs on a million-piece mailing.

The Mechanics of Postal Rate Increases

CPC rate increases have been regulated since 1998 with a Price-Cap formula for Lettermail. In 2002, the rate increase formula was ratified to not exceed two-thirds of the Consumer Price Index. Increases can be made no more than once a year, in January, and must be announced six months in advance in the Canada Gazette.

At the time of this writing, an additional increase is scheduled for 2006, which will raise the price another cent. As long as the rate of inflation continues to rise, direct mailers should plan on CPC rates following suit. Since CPC is Canada's seventh largest employer and operates one of the largest fleets of vehicles in the country, the rate increases begin to appear reasonable. In addition, deliverable addresses are a constantly moving target, experiencing an expansion rate of about 170,000 deliverable addresses annually. CPC has one of the lowest postal rates in the industrialized world while maintaining complete coverage of a very large country, second in geographic size only to Russia.

The Bottom Line

Direct mailing professionals should count on mail rates to keep on increasing. This means direct mailers need to get a better bang for their customers' promotional buck and mail smarter by constantly improving their:

- Target markets
- Capture of automation discounts
- Creative designs and offers

Better targeting means improving list management, data collection, analysis and response rates. There's always room for improved data cleansing so that more mail gets to the right destinations and is put in the hands of key business influencers. Second, since better targeting usually results in smaller-sized mailings, direct mailers are likely to lose some valuable automation discounts. This means that there is an opportunity for innovative ways to squeeze out automation discounts. Lastly, creative designs and offers always are important to future mailing success. Use good test marketing principles before rolling out expensive direct mail campaigns.

PAL POINT... For now, it's smart to just keep an ear to the ground about future postal rate increases. Position yourself as an industry resource and help navigate reasonable courses of action for your clients. Get ready because for better or worse, postal increases are a continuing reality.

6

Set Realistic Mailing Objectives

Know the goals of every project of yours and make sure they're realistic. For example, is it realistic to sell a $20,000 networking solution from a $1.50 mailing? No, but a $100 software program may be. How about a $2,000 furnace? Perhaps not, but getting prospects to visit an informational website or getting existing customers to schedule a $75 furnace cleaning certainly is.

What about selling a luxury car with a single mailing? Again, no! However, it is a reasonable goal to get potential buyers into showrooms for test-drives. Jaguar Canada did just this when their marketers sent 110,000 highly personalized direct mail packages to an upscale target audience. Those who test-drove a Jaguar as a result of this direct mail promotion were given a die cast model Jaguar worth $80. (Of course the out-of-pocket cost was less.) As a direct result, hundreds of automobiles were sold.

How do the economics of direct mail work for low-cost items? Let's consider magazine subscriptions, where the cost of acquiring a new subscriber is higher than the total first year's revenue. When you consider the lifetime value of customers, direct mail subscription programs make sense. If you keep track of all program results and associated costs, you will know your return on direct mail investment. As you experiment with new components and program design changes, you can always measure results against the control piece and make good promotional decisions.

Time Expectations

Consider the delivery method when preparing the mailing. A piece that is sent as Unaddressed Admail or Addressed Admail can take more time to be delivered because understandably CPC views the piece as having less priority than

Lettermail. There is no guarantee that an Admail piece will enter the system with the same urgency. If the piece must be delivered by or before a specific expiration date, then plan ahead and choose an appropriate postal service.

In today's fast-paced economy, most mailings are highly time sensitive and the critical production path may include a bottleneck that can hinder achieving intended in-home dates. Be aware of required production times and all appropriate cut off dates. It's important that direct mail production managers make their customers aware of material and supply lead times so that critical targets during the production process are consistently met.

Focus on Expected Results

Let's get back to the luxury car. Did you know that, on average, every young person who walks into a car dealership has $400,000 of lifetime purchases written on his or her forehead? This means that getting people into the dealer's door should be the goal of the direct marketer. If you modify your objective from "selling cars" to "getting qualified potential buyers into dealerships," you will experience better (and more realistic) results. Project champions should think of the lifetime value of a customer, regardless of whether the product is liquor, cars, credit cards, or almost anything else. Once the scope of the project is properly defined, all that needs to be done is good implementation.

What if you're trying to sell magazines? If you look at the cost of subscription acquisition as a percentage of the actual product itself you can set targets that have an acceptable payback period. Then, you will know an acceptable size budget and work within those constraints. Most direct mailings need to be profit motivated with an acceptable return generated from every investment.

7

Direct Mail Program Planning

Project lead times shrink every year. Effective data controls will increase the speed of your data processing and get your materials in the mail stream faster. Cost is more important than ever. Front-end data management will decrease data production time and save you money. Mailings that use multiple lists will benefit from back-end data analysis so future mailings can be smaller, yet achieve the same number of responses. Put all these ingredients together in an effective CRM (Customer Relationship Management) program.

Key Ingredients for Successful Programs

The first step in any direct mail project, regardless of whether it's part of a CRM program should be the identification of your target market and desired results. Many project designs would run better and cheaper if minor adjustments were made at the beginning of creative development. Therefore, a direct marketing technical team, with data processing, imaging, bindery, lettershop, and response management expertise should be present at all program development meetings.

Make your data file structure uniform and use industry standard media formats. Prior to handing off the project to your data house, create a data file layout. Without this, your supplier will need to decipher one, which takes time and increases your chances of error. A data file layout includes elements such as name and address components, list identifier codes, telephone numbers (for tandem telemarketing), account numbers, as well as

Tech Tip Establish a realistic critical path. Once a project's goals have been agreed upon, clearly communicate them to all appropriate people. Unless the internal and external business partners know your project's goals, their ability to help you is limited.

```
        SMR · Tytrek Group                              Page:  1
        Date & Time:  16/09/2005 5:02:09 PM

Layout for file:    gold_e.pdf           [ FLAT Text ]
   Record Length:   293

Record Quantity:    28,132

  Start      Length       Field Name      Field Type

  1          15           CUST_NO         C
  16         30           FIRSTNAME       C
  46         30           LASTNAME        C
  76         45           ADDRESS1        C
  121        45           ADDRESS2        C
  166        30           CITY            C
  196        5            PROV            C
  201        10           POSTAL_C        C
  211        12           ANN_DT          C
  223        12           REN_DT          C
  235        12           EXP_DT          C
  247        10           MEMBERSH        C
  257        2            FIN_LANG        C
  259        10           SMRID           C
  269        25           FILECODE        C
```

Sample file layout. (Courtesy SMR•Tytrek)

other demographic and psychographic pieces of information. Then, provide your supplier with detailed instructions (data specification logic) enabling programmers to clean up your database exactly the way you want.

Before beginning a direct mail CRM campaign, project champions need to start by clearly defining the desired response that they want from mail recipients. If getting people into a showroom is the goal, the program should be designed one way. If it's to get families to remove existing pizza magnets from their refrigerators, and put up yours instead, your program needs to be designed another way. If you're soliciting on the behalf of a nonprofit charitable organization, you will need yet a different set of goals.

Once goals are identified and agreed upon, it is the role of the project champion to ensure that continuity is built into a program. As in direct sales, where sales representatives need to call on prospects seven times on average before reaching the first sale, direct mail isn't too different. While some people will respond to the first piece of mail they receive, many others need to be exposed to the message several times before they feel compelled to take the desired action. "One-Shot-Charlie" type mailings rarely influence enough people the first time to make the program cost-effective. Start-up costs, which may include list acquisition, design costs, and production inefficiencies, need to be amortized over repeat mailings to be cost-effective.

An Example

In the late 1990s, a pharmaceutical company had ambitions of developing a newsletter full of useful information targeted toward people suffering from a specific allergy-related medical problem. The pharmaceutical company didn't know much about direct mail design, but at least they did know they wanted subscription growth, market awareness, sales generation, and measurable results. To start with, they had a fledgling database of about 15,000 carefully selected recipients, but no realistic knowledge of where the program could go and what it could be used to achieve. The company thought that the information-laden newsletter could trigger sales and retain existing customers, but they weren't sure. They contracted the project out to one of the authors, who helped them design a complete direct mail loop that included mail, analysis, redesign, re-mail, more analysis, and so forth.

The results were tracked through a few complete cycles, and the pharmaceutical company discovered exactly what information each recipient needed. Then, they were able to appropriately customize the newsletter for individual reader. The company solicited feedback in several ways, but the most effective method was discovered to be a perforated reply card. Soon all their newsletters contained this response device. Results were tracked and within a few short months, the company had gathered a mountain of information from the newsletter, website, and other advertising activities. In all, they captured data for 200,000 targeted recipients, after removing duplicate and undeliverable records. This information was captured, kept current and within a short period of time became a valuable source of business.

Additionally, the author's company was solicited for design advice. As a result, some highly effective promotional pieces were developed and distributed to segments of the client's self-developed "house" data file, which further augmented the program's success. To streamline the process of capturing information written on returned reply cards, the company used inside/outside inkjet imaging technology, which reduced the amount of handwriting needing to be read. Better information led to better results, which in turn led to better information. This is the kind of vicious cycle that clients like.

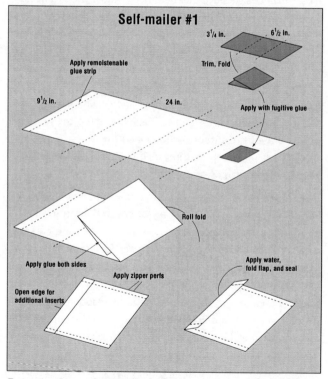

Example of how a self-mailer is designed. (Courtesy SMR•Tytrek)

Now that they've tasted real success, this pharmaceutical company intends on continuing this database effort, in addition to doing everything else right on the list acquisition and testing side.

Here's a last footnote regarding this pharmaceutical company. Company representatives asked themselves how they could parlay the success of this program to other products and areas of their company. The goal no longer was whether direct mail would work, but how they can best showcase total company strengths to achieve goals across other business units as well. They were so pleased with their results that they rolled out similar programs in other drug areas with much larger sales volumes and much more ambitious mailing sizes. These types of excellent results are a byproduct of well-thought-out job planning early in the development of the project.

PAL POINT... Repetition, two-way communication, and program continuity are at the core of an effective CRM (customer relationship marketing) program. It's vital that direct marketers think about lifetime relationships as they conceive and manage their various projects. How can a solicitation for a magazine at an 80% discount pay for itself unless a relationship with a subscriber is maintained beyond the trial membership period? Not surprisingly, it can't. Repetitive contact is what makes many types of mailings pay off. Seasoned direct mailing professionals usually think of direct mail programs in terms of years, not weeks or months. Only then are their expectations realistic and successful.

Account Management

If you enjoy working with a wide variety of people, crave being in the center of the action, and thrive in a fast-paced work environment, then direct mail account management may be just your ticket. Salespeople bring in the work. Production makes it happen. Account managers ensure that everything is done right and on time. Although a lot of people with different functional responsibilities need to work in harmony to produce direct mail jobs on time and on budget, let's focus on account management. This role in direct mail services is quite different than in most other industries.

Overview

Account managers are a vital communication link between the customer and internal production. All requests from customers should be channeled through this department. A good policy is to not allow work to be scheduled without first being assigned an account manager.

To succeed, account managers must:
- Have a complete understanding of the client job specifications
- Communicate clearly and effectively, both verbally and in writing
- Be able to process all detailed, complex ideas and requests
- Manage a multitude of jobs, processes, and paperwork in a timely and organized manner
- Follow a job's progress throughout the production process
- Immediately notify sales representatives and other key personnel of any delays or significant challenges

Account managers should think of their function as being both "vendor" and "customer" to their internal and external customers. As a "customer," account managers must treat everyone with dignity and respect and be fully prepared when discussing or handing off jobs. They should put all requests or job changes in writing and ask for the same in return. When problems occur, it is important to keep the management team fully aware of what is happening.

As a "vendor," account managers can never forget that since they are authorized representatives of their employer they must treat all customers with dignity and respect. They should request all information or specifications in writing and provide the same. Job processing documentation must be prepared and kept up-to-date so that nothing falls through the cracks. When problems occur, it's much better to let your customers know sooner than later, especially if delivery dates are in jeopardy. And, like a good salesperson, it is important to know your customers' goals and work to achieve them in partnership.

Take Personal Responsibility

An account management reality is that some customers require more involvement than others. Some customers ask their assigned account managers to provide more support and marketing guidance in conjunction with project management tasks. Seasoned account managers know that each client has different expectations. To provide the right amount of support, account managers should look to the sales representatives that they work with for guidance.

It is important to keep in mind that each job and client is the ultimate responsibility of the assigned account manager. Account managers must check the quality of the jobs throughout each stage of the manufacturing process. Account managers function as the "eyes and ears" for their customers while their jobs are in house. The levels of attention that account managers pay to their jobs and the type of communication style that they use will ultimately determine the success or failure of the customer relationship. Anticipating potential problems and following up on every promise and concern is essential to ensuring customer satisfaction. Decision-making speed and consistent good judgment are key success factors.

Consider yourself and your company to be in partnership with your customers. Learn what their goals are and work to achieve them. Providing quality account management and support services go a long way toward creating extended profitable relationships. Perhaps many customers will name your company as their preferred vendor.

Account managers must be available to their customers. It is very important that they quickly and courteously respond to telephone messages, pages, and emails. Unresponsiveness is extremely frustrating to customers, destroys confidence, and threatens business relationships—even long-term ones. Be diligent in returning all communications in a timely manner.

Information and Specifications

When receiving job instructions and specifications, account managers must invest the proper amount of time to completely understand each project. It is important that they receive complete written instructions from the client. If they are missing, it is their responsibility to get them. Without consistent and accurate data, it is impossible to do a good job. The account management team leader should develop written procedures and create a job checklist to help account managers make sure that they have all the detailed information they need. As your company's services evolve, these procedures and checklists should be updated as necessary.

It is the duty of the account manager to fully understand every job on which he or she works. This means understanding the ultimate goal or output of each request. Without a complete understanding of the "final destination," it is difficult to produce the job correctly or get it there on time. It is critical that account managers clearly and accurately interpret job information and hand off jobs to other departments with unambiguous directions. Particular attention should be paid to communicating any expectations that are unique to the job. When dealing with internal data service departments, an easy and effective way to communicate job requirements is to use flowcharts. These flowcharts can be either simple or elaborate depending upon the processes required.

Job Changes

In the direct mail industry, change is a constant. While working on jobs, frequently you will receive requests to change or modify the original order. It is very important for these changes to be submitted in writing and they should be clear, understandable, and plainly written. Since customer relationships are so important, avoid verbal changes whenever possible. Of utmost importance, make sure your internal and external clients know that changes or modifications can cause the project to be delayed and may increase costs. You may need to renegotiate the due date and/or job pricing. Don't forget to involve the salesperson in this process, modify all internal paperwork, and properly redistribute the revised job order. Since more internal coordination is necessary, errors are more likely when job changes occur than when they don't. So, try to get it right the first time.

At the outset of any job, make sure you and all involved are prepared for changes that may occur in the process. Be upfront with the production team regarding the importance of the information needed to run the job on time and accurately. Steer clear of any pitfalls or hurdles that may crop up that impose changes in deadline and accuracy.

Provide daily updates for clients because shared knowledge greatly helps open communication. Potential production problems will be exposed before they occur. This process will keep all abreast of necessary action items and timelines. In the event that issues arise, be proactive. Don't wait until the last moment to begin the communication process.

Production meetings are important to the overall progress of any job. When issues arise in the supply chain or the status of a key piece of machinery it is imperative that the account representative be aware and able to pass that information along to the client with accuracy. However, be mindful of the impact of internal issues so that when relaying the details to the client there is a clear understanding of what those issues mean in regards to the timing and quality of the job.

PAL POINT... Change is an inevitable part of direct mail account management. It is especially important that account managers think about how requested changes will affect production, all the while looking for unexpected side effects. Usually it is better to delay a job in order to be certain it is correct than to run the risk of producing it incorrectly.

Communication

Success in the direct mail world depends on choosing the right paper, layout, printing, binding, and personalization methods, right? Is this all? Not unless you want to ignore the most valuable key success factor: good communication.

Today's direct mail professionals are stretched so thinly that they must rely on their suppliers to guide them through the complicated buying process. The best direct mail companies help customers maneuver around landmines and achieve their business goals. Let your partners help you in the same way. In addition to simply faxing over job specifications, pick up the phone and discuss your project. Good communication allows you to reduce costs, eliminate frustration, and be a hero in the eyes of your customers.

If direct mailing services customers supply all their vendors (up and down the direct mail supply chain) with accurate and timely information, everyone's lives will be less stressful. The number of problems will be reduced, customer satisfaction will rise, production costs will be lower, and profits will be higher. When job specifications are unclear, questions go unanswered and production problems increase exponentially.

Data processing companies, lettershops, and binderies want to be valuable information resources for their customers, but effective two-way information flow is needed to achieve this lofty goal. Before direct mail professionals can present alternative solutions to their customers, they need information about a job's end-use. They need to know the minutia of your job to be of the greatest value to you. In short, your suppliers depend on good communication and information flow.

Begin with the End in Mind

The best printing layout isn't necessarily the most efficient mail or bindery layout. For example, if a job is bindery-intensive, it may be in the mailer's best interest to change the layout to save on outsourcing costs and production time. Sometimes one-up layouts are best, and sometimes multiple-up ones are best. Working in a vacuum can be terribly inefficient and costly.

Minor product design changes might allow machines to run faster and reduce spoilage. The bottom line? There are definitely times when a little more should be spent on printing to save in the bindery or lettershop, or vice versa. But this discovery process can only start with good two-way communication. Work backwards through the supply chain to ensure product and process efficiency.

Scheduling

Direct mail project leaders shouldn't wait until their job is printed before contacting their lettershop or bindery representative. Scheduling conflicts are a way of life in the direct mail world, and the best way to ensure that your due date is met is to schedule your job well in advance. Good suppliers of direct mail services know that problems happen and do their best to accommodate minor changes to schedules.

When Sending a Job

Before placing a job, write an instruction sheet for each supplier explaining what you want done, along with a sample. You may not know when or how this minor time investment will help you, but it will. No one is as familiar with your requirements as you are, and what seems obvious to you may not be to someone else. Purchase orders are certainly preferred, but at the very least, describe what operations need to be done and define success. Think of your job from the perspective of someone who has never heard of your client and doesn't know what items are on the "must" list.

It's uncomfortable for a manufacturing company to have an important production question regarding a rush job and not be able to get an answer. When in this awkward position, suppliers have two choices: either wait for information and miss the deadline or make an unauthorized production decision. Either way, they risk incurring the wrath of their customers if they are wrong. Jobs with quick turnaround times and poorly communicated instructions are disasters waiting to happen.

PAL POINT... Help your supply chain help you. In today's fast-paced business environment, one unplanned detail can break the proverbial camel's back. Good communication with all involved companies will make your life easier and increase your profits in the hectic direct mail world.

Testing

One of the truest maxims of the direct mail business is: "test, test and then test some more." Some of the most effective direct marketers seem to be decidedly understated about the importance of creative. They know that great results don't necessarily follow from the flashiest or most graphically challenging campaigns. Instead, if a dull looking campaign performs better during a test, they chuck the award winner and follow the pieces with better results.

If this sounds paradoxical, it shouldn't. Direct marketing isn't about winning "Cassies," "Daveys," or any other type of industry award. Rather, it's about being detached enough to deemphasize one's own design preferences and having the discipline to stick with what works. If your superb looking new creative design doesn't out-pull the control product, you should either change it and try again or put the concept out to pasture. In direct mail the only thing that counts is results. Woe is to the direct marketer who ignores this time-tested lesson. The best continuing direct mail programs are those that constantly test a single changing condition and incorporate the changes that work and setting aside the ones that

Tech Tip

Developing and implementing a continual testing strategy is critical to the success of high volume mailing campaigns. Personalization, manufacturing costs and mailing class choices are all significant factors. Just as you need to test the effectiveness of postal code versus letter carrier presort rates, consider testing different levels of personalization. Some companies have discovered that avoiding unattractive carrier route markings is the best way to increase profits. Some people have learned that deeper levels of mail customization do the same.

don't. In this way, smart marketers achieve the best performing pieces with repeatable results.

Mechanics of Testing

Testing is an involved process where creative and/or physical components of a piece are altered to determine the impact of that particular variation in relation to overall response. Testing should only be done on one element of a project at a time. For example, to test the style of envelope, don't change the color or printing process. To test the offer, don't change the wording or the package. Be very specific with each aspect of the piece so that results can be effectively measured based on one particular variation.

Test across in different geographic/socioeconomic areas. A program that generates a good response within an urban area may have an entirely different result out in the country. Western Canadian markets might test differently from the Maritime Provinces. Many other factors can affect results if the testing pool is not carefully selected.

When your database size is relatively small, a rule of thumb is to test no less than 10% of your list. Obviously, a larger testing percentage will yield a more accurate preview of future results. For larger mailings, of a million pieces or more, tests in the 15,000–20,000 piece ranges should be sufficient.

The primary reason for testing is to drive future profits. Physical component costs are critical. Keep in mind that if a small bump in response rate doesn't offset the increase materials and production costs, it isn't worth it (in most cases).

Industry legend David Olgivy describes the testing process this way in *Olgivy on Advertising:*

> You can test every variable in your mailings and
> determine exactly its effect on your sales. But
> because you can only test one variable at a time,

you cannot afford to test them all. So you have to choose which to test. Experienced practitioners always test some variables, but seldom those that experience has taught them make little difference in results. Next to the positioning of your product, the most important variables to be tested are pricing, terms of payment, premiums, and the format of your mailing.

Asking for the full price and cash with the order will reduce the number of people who respond. But it may turn up more customers who are likely to stay with you over the years. Only testing will tell. The more you test, the more profitable your direct mail will become.

Once you have evolved a mailing that produces profitable results, treat it as a "control" and start testing ways to beat it. Try adding a premium, or putting in an expiration date, or adding enclosures—like a personalized letter from your president. They cost money, but if they increase your profit, why worry?

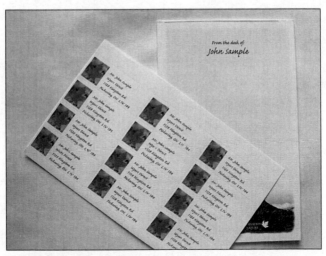

Sample of personalized pad and mailing labels combined as a premium. (Courtesy Wyers Direct)

Sometimes an expensive control can be made less expensive without reducing your orders. You can test a smaller mailing piece, or eliminate the brochure altogether. You may be in for a pleasant surprise. Less can be more.

PAL POINT... Don't assume anything. Test every component of your mailing. Test the envelope copy, colour, and graphics. Test inserts, letter copy, letter length, headlines, signatures, messages, and offers. Test fonts, graphics, premiums, attachments, bindery processes, and labels. Test different lists, demographics, and psychographics. Don't assume. *Test.*

Quality Assurance

Without quality, you don't have a product. Successful direct mail service providers define, measure, audit, and analyze quality. Although admittedly a daunting task, designing effective quality assurance systems and procedures is well worth the effort. Before outsourcing your next direct mail job, ask existing and potential suppliers about their approach to quality assurance. You will make better outsourcing decisions.

Quality involves everyone within an organization—from production workers to company presidents. Quality is not what customers expect; it's what manufacturers inspect. The backbone of a good quality assurance program is accountability. If employees believe that their mistakes either don't matter or will be caught by other people, complacency and lack of attention to detail will be the logical result. Quality assurance is a balancing act. When taken to ridiculous levels, unrealistic quality fanaticism kills output and profitability.

One challenge the direct mail production industry faces is that every piece of mail is different. Therefore, we must question everything. If operators don't see a barcode, they need to look at the production docket to see if it's missing. If they see a barcode, they also need to look at the production docket to verify image positioning. Get the point? Either way they've got to look at the production docket. Direct mail production occurs in a variable job shop manufacturing environment. This is quite different from our cousins in the printing and binding industries. There, conformity is the goal and success depends on every piece being the same. Those of us in direct mail production deal with constantly changing parameters, which is exactly the opposite of stasis.

Quality Assurance Needs Great Information Systems

A company's choice of job definition/production workflow software is critically important to future success. Consistent product quality depends on accurate job definitions and unambiguous communication between departments. High-volume mail service providers need integrated software systems that:

- Disseminate the right information to the right departments
- Determine the shortest manufacturing critical paths
- Integrate production schedules with other work in house
- Track material flow
- Monitor production on a real-time basis

No two customers are alike. People provide information in different ways and it's up to account managers to get varying information into a standard, familiar format, easily understood by everyone. Good software standardizes and disperses customer instructions to the right people throughout a manufacturing facility.

Operating procedures are also necessary and can prevent a major headache. For example, most financial services companies offer different credit card interest rates to people with different credit ratings. This means that production employees need to be extremely careful that all components of a mailing contain the same rate offer. Employees should have the power to halt production to avoid these kinds of situations.

Data Audit

Your mailing services company should sample converted data before beginning production. These "data audits," often referred to as dumps and counts, usually involve random sampling by extracting records from the outgoing data file and examining them for conformity to customer expectations. Everything is checked including data field content (i.e., Postal Code, customer ID, ordering history, etc), upper and lower case use, data truncation, and so forth.

If a data audit reveals a problem, it is important to determine where it occurred. Most mail houses start at the end of the data conversion process and work backwards by examining the printing program, output file (post-data conversion) and input file (pre-data conversion)—in that order. For example, if a data audit reveals a truncating problem, we may discover that a computer operator picked up data from byte positions 15 to 20 instead of from 15 to 30. Although fixing a problem such as this consumes additional resources, at least the mailing will not have been produced wrong.

Interval Sampling

It is hard to imagine a quality assurance program without good sampling and inspection procedures. Standards must be defined in all production departments and may differ, even within the same job. Some operations are susceptible to manufacturing problems and high spoilage rates while others run great for days, weeks, and months on end. Understandably, problem-prone manufacturing areas require more frequent sample inspection. Customer requirements and job quantities also are important factors in determining appropriate sampling intervals.

Quality assurance needs machine operators armed with clearly written the production docket regarding sampling frequency and product expectations. These operators are the frontlines that pull samples, inspect the work, and record their findings. The next quality assurance layer involves production monitors who constantly inspect recent sample pulls. Stage three involves gathering, examining, recording, and storing samples. The last step is the account manager who shoulders ultimate responsibility for customer expectation compliance.

Analysis: Seeing the Big Picture

Deconstructing problems and analyzing results are vital to manufacturing performance and customer satisfaction. Good companies analyze production data and determine whether overall quality is trending in the right direction. Not only do they examine historical data, they consider other information such as out-of-pocket rework costs, wasted production hours, and percentage of on-time deliveries.

Analysis allows mailing service providers to recognize when error patterns emerge. If errors are sporadically dispersed throughout a plant, they're probably OK. However, detectable patterns of problems may be indicative of a systemic breakdown somewhere. Regardless, it's important to study available data and make better decisions based on past history.

The two most dangerous types of employees are those who can't follow instructions and those who can only follow instructions. It's unrealistic to believe that you or anyone else can write procedures that will cover all or even most manufacturing contingencies. The bottom line is that job shop manufacturers need people who can think.

PAL POINT... Within each of the authors' companies, there is the saying "if you find your mistake, it's not a mistake." The logical corollary is this: "If someone else finds your mistake, then it's a mistake." Quality assurance begins with each individual and radiates throughout an organization. It requires well-thought-out management procedures and information technologies. No matter which tools are best suited for a particular manufacturing facility, they must improve job definition, measurement, auditing, and analysis. Quality assurance helps companies keep their promises. Isn't this the point of being in business?

Privacy Issues

Effective direct marketing requires tailoring messages to the individual needs, wants, and requirements of consumers. To effectively communicate along these lines requires personal information about consumers. The power of this information enables the direct marketer to accurately target consumer habits, demands and trends. This is one of the most powerful tools available to the marketing industry. However, there is a tremendous level of responsibility and legal obligation that comes along with many types of data, especially financial.

The general consumer is more conscious and increasingly nervous about privacy issues. People don't want to give out their name or reveal their habits. They are growing more apprehensive about the information companies are mining and storing. However, these trends should not restrain a company from properly using this data for the consumers benefit as long as careful measures are taken to establish, implement, and enforce privacy policies.

Privacy Legislation Guidelines

The Personal Information Protection and Electronic Documents Act (PIPEDA) stipulates guidelines for private and public organizations in the collection, use, and storage of consumer information. Ultimately suppliers are held responsible for the databases they acquire, manipulate, and retain for their clients. The law demands that companies handle sensitive information in a respectful and highly secure environment. This is a serious issue that demands serious attention.

PIPEDA was originally designed to regulate the collection, use, and disclosure of federally monitored institutions in financial and telecommunications industries. This act has been extended to encompass retail, publishing, service, and manufacturing industries as regulated by province. Direct mail marketing companies should be familiar with these laws and regulations while taking necessary steps to comply.

Privacy Policy

Accurate databases are an essential tool in effective direct mail marketing. Ultimately suppliers are responsible for these databases, including how they are stored and manipulated for their clients. Companies must demonstrate a privacy policy that plainly specifies how the direct mail marketer is safely and securely storing and using this information. This policy must be clearly and explicitly communicated. Failure to take the issue seriously could quickly and easily result in a loss of revenue, credibility, and ultimately the right to do business.

PAL POINT... This particular issue is gravely important while the information used is a vital resource in effectively doing business. Establish the necessary policies. Implement the tools and resources to manage these policies. And openly disclose these policies and procedures whenever and wherever necessary to insure they are clearly communicated and applied.

SECTION 2
Direct Mail Pre-Production

Production-Friendly Direct Mail Layouts

There's a time and place for eye-popping unusual direct mail designs, but often direct mailing professionals need to produce good projects at the lowest possible cost. Achieving production efficiencies depends on starting with machine capabilities firmly in mind and working backward to arrive at production-friendly layouts. For example, when planning laser-personalized direct mail projects, pay attention to mailing equipment limitations, because some formats are more conducive to long production runs than others. It is so easy for designers to wistfully add a ¼ in. (6 mm) here and ⅛ in. (3 mm)there without realizing they're dramatically increasing their production costs.

Production-unfriendly layouts can waste a lot of paper, machine time, effort and energy, while increasing manufacturing costs and blowing deadlines. Unless there's a very good reason to do otherwise, high-volume mailing professionals should design their projects so they conform to common machine specifications.

Common Press Sizes

Some people think that efficient production is limited to the printing press's cylinder circumference divided by two, which, in the case with most common direct mail machine (22 in. , 559 mm), results in an 11-in. (279-mm) cutoff. This is wrong. A cut-off of 7⅓ in. (186 mm) or 5½ in. (140 mm) is just as

Efficient Direct Mail Cutoff Sizes

Inches	Millimeters
5½	140
5⅗	142
5⅔	144
7	178
7⅓	186
8½	216
9⅓	237
11	279
14	356
17	432
22	559
28	711

The most common cylinder circumference sizes used in direct mail is 17½ in. (445 mm). The circumference of the printing press cylinder determines efficient cutoff sizes. For example, a cylinder with a 28-in. (711-mm) circumference is efficient for 14-in. products (28 ÷ 2), 9⅓-in. (28 ÷ 3) and 7-in. (28 ÷ 4). If your direct mail piece needs to be just a little taller than 8½ in., you might as well design it having a height of 9⅓ in., instead of 8¾ in. or any other production-unfriendly size. If you make a mistake and design a piece with a height of 9½ in., then you must use an 11-in. form, which wastes 13.6% of the available paper and slows down production as well.

efficient on a 22-in. cylinder. When planning product sizes, take your cylinder's circumference and divide evenly. Just because 11-in. products are so prevalent doesn't mean you have to limit yourself to this size; 14 in. (356 mm), 17 in. (432 mm) and all their derivative sizes are just as efficient to produce.

Production Inefficiencies Caused by Takeout

A lot of direct mail work is finished on Bowie-style document conversion machines. Two important settings on document converters determine: (1) how far paper advances, and (2) how much "takeout" is required.

A major production bottleneck is knife-cutting speed. If an 11-in. (279-mm) form without bleeds is being produced on a 22-in. (559-mm) circumference cylinder, the knife only needs to make one cut per form. However, if you have a production-unfriendly format of 9½ in. (241 mm) for example, you need 1½-in. (38-mm) takeout between forms. This requires the knife to travel twice, slowing down production by at least 30%. Moreover, you'll be wasting about 15% of your time on printing presses and laser imagers because only 19 in. (483 mm) of the available 22-in. circumference will be actually imaged. Bottom line: It's very important to avoid takeouts when designing high-volume mail projects.

The width of the form is important too. The maximum roll width on most laser imaging machines is 18 in. (457 mm). After allowing for two ½-in. (13-mm) pin-feed strips, designers have a 17-in. (432-mm) roll width available for image use. Eliminat-

Tech Tip Combining black-only printing with holograms and Label-Aire applications may be a good way to achieve the design flexibility you need without sacrificing production speed.

ing paper width roll waste is easy—just decrease the width of the paper roll. (Note: Ordering special roll sizes from the mill may cost more and take longer to receive.) However, you're paying for production on 18-in.-wide machines, meaning that even though you're only using a 15-in. (381-mm) roll, you're still paying 18-in. machine rates for both printing presses and laser imagers. As with height, don't forget you can run your forms multiple-wide. In the case of an 18-in. roll (17-in. image area), 17-, 8½-, and 5⅔-in.-wide (432-, 216-, and 144-mm-wide) forms all maximize roll width.

Image Rotation: An Example of a 16% Productivity Gain

In certain circumstances, rotating your image 90° will save you time and money. Consider a 17-in.-tall form that is 7⅓ in. wide. If you run this project two-up on a 17-in. circumference cylinder, you will need a 15⅔-in.-wide paper roll (7⅓ in. × 2, plus 1 in. for pin-feed holes). For every 17 in. of paper length, you'll get two forms out. Instead, rotate your image

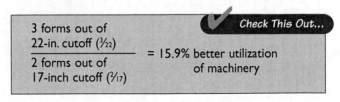

$$\frac{\text{3 forms out of 22-in. cutoff } (^3\!/_{22})}{\text{2 forms out of 17-inch cutoff } (^2\!/_{17})} = 15.9\% \text{ better utilization of machinery}$$

Check This Out...

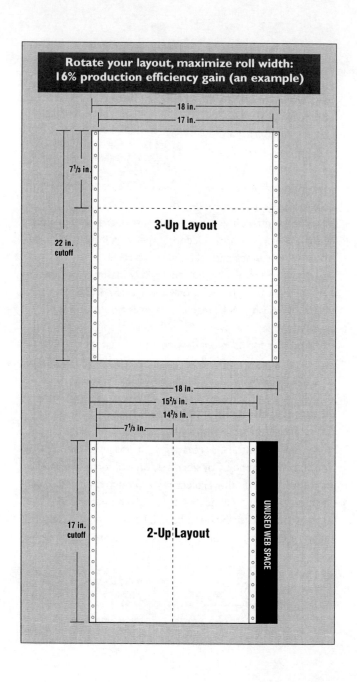

90° to get three forms out of a 22-in. cylinder—a perfect fit resulting in a productivity gain of nearly 16%.

There are other benefits, too. For example, you'll be folding your forms with the paper grain, which makes a significant quality difference on heavier stocks. And, you're being charged for less printing footage while maximizing the width of the machine. If you're paying your laser personalization services company $1.50/M an inch, you will now get a form every 7$\frac{1}{3}$ in. (186 mm) instead of every 8$\frac{1}{2}$ in. (216 mm), which amounts to roughly $1.75/M in laser imaging and $1.00/M in printing costs. In addition, there's the chance that ordering a special roll width will increase your paper costs a bit as well. Let's put it all together. Rotating the image and shifting production to a 22-in. circumference cylinder will likely save you between $3/M and $4/M without sacrificing any image quality.

The most common sheet laser sizes are 11×17 in. (279×432 mm) and 14×17 in. (356×432 mm) with the obvious relationship to a standard business letter at 8$\frac{1}{2}$×11 in. Here too, nonstandard pieces should be reviewed carefully in order to obtain the best possible production fit and cost combination.

Bleeds are quite common in the printing world and sometimes are not given a second thought on larger press sheets. However, when planning both sheet and continuous laser letters and applications, bleeds need to be planned for early in the production process since sheet sizes can be restrictive.

Also important is how you finish your projects. For example, assume you need an 8$\frac{1}{2}$×11-in. (216×279-mm) personalized letter and a 3$\frac{1}{2}$×8$\frac{1}{2}$-in. (89×216-mm) reply device. If you run it on a 14-in. (356-mm) form, gatefold it and slit it to the head, you will get a personalized letter and a freestanding, nested personalized reply device. Although gate folding costs more than standard folding, it is far less expensive than outsourcing a matched mailing, with far fewer headaches. If you are producing a toner-only form, then offset printing isn't needed, removing cutoff limitations.

PAL POINT... There are a lot of direct mail machines out there. For our purposes, we've limited our discussions to the most widely available equipment. If you look hard enough, you could find other pieces of equipment with different specs, but these are few and far between and you may find them to be priced higher and a capacity limitation.

Choose the Right Paper

The right paper choices can often impact the success of a direct mail campaign. Paper needs to be considered early on in the planning process. If your selection is too thin or thick, it may exceed specifications on the most efficient machines. If it is too expensive, it might not yield the best profits. And worst of all, it might not even be available in the size and quantity required at the time you need it.

Take into account the end use of the paper. If the piece is expected to be repeatedly used by the consumer, your paper selection may need to be more durable. If it is going to have a short shelf life, perhaps a one-time promotional flyer, an inexpensive #3 stock may yield the best financial perform-ance. If the material is going to have sample items attached, glues must be compatible with the stock and strength again becomes an issue.

Often designers will choose a paper that has a specific texture. Textured papers are commonplace in printing now. However, they may be cost-prohibitive and unnecessary in achieving the desired result. Quite often it is possible to achieve a par-ticular texture effect in the process rather than in the paper. Think through the entire manufacturing process and choose an appropriate paper stock.

Availability and size restric-tions are often imposed on the process as well. As indi-cated earlier, what may be most desirable may not be readily available. In the case of time-sensitive communi-

Tech Tip Consider the types of processes the paper must endure before completion. Printers know how different toners and dies affect paper. Use this knowledge to match the job with the correct type of paper. The amount and type of folds in a piece should help determine stock durability and grain direction.

cations, consider ease of procurement. Some papers are only produced in particular sizes. Take the entire process into account before making a choice that may not easily print or fold to the intended size.

Grain direction can hinder job timing and quality. Many papers don't fold well against the grain. Recycled stocks that lack a consistent grain direction usually don't absorb inks or glues as well as virgin stocks. If the imaging process is digital instead of conventional offset printing, make sure toner will properly adhere to your paper. If a reply form needs to be run through a laser printer later, make sure that previously applied toner, ink, coatings and glues are all heat resistant. In short, variables can be numerous and each has a potential impact on job success.

PAL POINT... Paper choices can make or break the budget. If there is any doubt in what the best choice may be then run sample tests on the desired stocks as well as on alternative stocks. It just may reveal that what is preferred will not be as cost-effective, durable, or attractive as an alternative stock. The proof is in the output.

Postal-Friendly Envelope Design

Direct mail projects won't be successful unless they're well planned. This includes paying attention to every detail, right down to individual mail components. Envelope selection is very important for two reasons: marketing effectiveness and production efficiency. With so much marketplace emphasis on cost containment, we'll concentrate on production efficiencies today.

Choose the right envelope for your next mailing. With proper training, direct mail project managers are able to foresee and avoid most envelope-related problems.

Window Envelopes

When a mailing suffers from poor production rates, the envelope window is often the culprit. Direct mail production companies prefer envelopes with cellophane windows instead of "open" (cellophane-less) ones because they are less susceptible to having inserts catch and rip on the windows. Even if open envelopes successfully make it through letter-shop production, they are still more likely to get caught in

Sample window envelope. (Courtesy Wyers Direct)

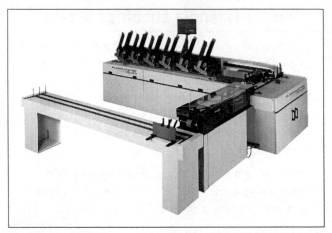

FlowMaster 12000 inserter. (Courtesy Sure-Feed Engineering, Inc.)

Canada Post Corporation (CPC) processing equipment than their cellophane counterparts. Open envelopes cost a bit less, but their increased production risk almost always outweighs this insignificant benefit.

Side-Seam vs. V-Style Envelopes

For large- volume jobs running on high-speed inserting equipment, choose side seam style envelopes with flat flaps. The distance that these flaps must travel during the opening and sealing processes determines production rates. Although

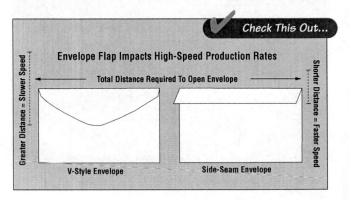

side-seam envelopes cost a bit more, associated production savings are more than enough compensation to lower your project's overall cost.

Tap Test

To qualify for postal discounts, addressed inserts must properly lie within their envelopes. Mailings need to pass a "tap" test in which the postal information (name, address, walk, and month codes) remains fully exposed as sealed samples are tapped from the bottom and both sides, jogging all contents in three directions. As each side is tapped, all address information must remain visible through the window with a $\frac{1}{8}$-in. (3-mm) clearance.

Although always important, this tap test is especially critical for thick mailings. Envelopes need to be opened wider than usual to accommodate a lot of inserted material. Since this mechanical action temporarily reduces envelope width by pulling in the upper corners, production rates usually depend on slightly undersized insert widths. However, undersized inserts shift more within sealed envelopes, making the left-right tap test increasingly important as mailings get thicker.

Envelope Potpourri

- Make sure your envelope manufacturer packs their products tightly. If letter shops are forced to use sagging, bowing, or otherwise imperfect envelopes, turnaround times, production costs and spoilage rates will be disappointing.

Tech Tip

For wet-applied "live" stamp jobs, make sure your lettershop is careful about moisture seepage because remoistenable glue strips can be unintentionally activated. Pressure-sensitive stamps eliminate this risk and are highly preferred.

- To qualify for maximum postal discounts, envelopes must comply with CPC aspect ratio standards. Although most standard envelope sizes comply, still it's best to confirm before beginning unusual-sized projects.
- If you want to use an envelope size larger than 6×9 in. (152×229 mm), choose oversized envelopes with flaps running lengthwise so that your mailing can be automatically inserted.
- Envelope coatings can cause adhesion problems. Adhesive technology is part art and part science. The only way to be certain that glue and inkjet ink will properly adhere to coated surfaces is to run tests before beginning production.

PAL POINT... Be careful when using old envelopes. Remoistenable glue is formulated to react quickly to the presence of moisture and may dry out if too much time passes before use.

Data Processing: Format and Record Layout

16

Smooth data processing can make all the difference between successful and unsuccessful mailing campaigns. Although technological advances have dramatically changed the direct mail landscape, cost-effective mailing programs still begin with good front-end data management.

Direct mail's future has never been brighter. Squarely in the sites of many electronic media options, the demand for direct mail is still increasing because it is non-invasive, user-friendly, reliable, and highly effective. Managing the complicated front-end data processing procedure under severe time constraints is an important key success factor in today's fast-paced business environment. Project managers should rely on their direct mail services company for data preparation expertise and involve them early in the design phase of any job.

The road to data preparation hell is paved with good intentions. Although large-volume mailing customers often try to process their data to a particular mailing company's standards, rarely is much time or money saved; instead, duplication of effort occurs. Out of necessity, most sophisticated direct mailing services companies have developed "house" data formats, which allows incoming data to be formatted only once, no matter which machines are required for production. From a client's perspective, conforming data to a mailing company's house format may appear to be easy, but it usually isn't.

Data Formats

Customers that send PC-based word processing or spreadsheet files should make sure that all their data components can be automatically parsed out. Although Word and Excel files may at first glance look like they're properly formatted, minor inconsistencies in line breaks, character spacing, and field positioning will require new programming code to be written. Most anomalies can be fixed and corrected, but mailer and client should get together early in the production planning process to reduce database processing time and aggravation. Instead of concentrating on who should do the data processing, a better approach is to focus on saving time and money, regardless of which company does the work. Again, good communication will determine the most cost-efficient and effective course of action.

Tech Tip If ASCII or database formats are used, once again software most likely will need to be written to find line and record breaks and prepare the data for postal presorts and address verification. While it's possible to put most lists in proper mailing condition, some hard-to-use files require a lot of programming time and subsequently cost a lot of money.

Most record layouts are preferred in a database file such as a .dbf, or MS Access file format. These files are automatically parsed where needed and typically contain a legend. It is possible and easy to translate most MS Excel files into MS Access files. However, do be mindful that the legends are often truncated and need to be edited so that the label for that field is accurately communicated. Text files (i.e., .txt and .csv) are also acceptable but do cause translation issues on the receiving end. Text files need to be delineated by tabs for optimum translation capabilities. Comma delineated text files typically require more programmer interaction, thus increasing the cost of preparing the list for use.

Data Manipulation

Splitting large files into smaller ones may reduce postal discounts. Assume you are mailing offers to prospective credit card applicants and are segmenting your database into four different categories of credit worthiness. If the job is processed in four lots instead of one, extra data processing will be required and postal discounts will decrease, unless the job is commingled prior to mail stream entry. If the components (envelope, letter, BRE, etc.) are the same for all four groups and the offer can be coded into specific fields, then the whole job should be processed and mailed in its entirety, saving a lot of postage. CPC does allow for staggered mailings; however, a Statement of Mailing must be included and all postage paid up front for the entire job.

On the other hand, if separate files are combined into one big file and field codes are stripped out, it will be difficult to appropriately match records and variable copy. If a mailing has physically different components (size, colours, shape, etc.) and the combined data files no longer have unique field and record break indicators, matching the right record and offer may not be possible.

If the job is run multiple-up, the data must be processed in an appropriate order. "East/West" imaging (first name left, next name right, etc.) will cause problems because the stacks will be out of order after final trimming. Instead, "north-south" ordering allows jobs to be processed, separated and married with the job ending up in proper mailing sequence. Bundle breaking is applicable when other auxiliary functions such as match mailings will be performed.

Presorting

Mailings need to be processed through CPC-approved Letter Carrier Presort (LCP) software. This process verifies the address bears a valid postal code and properly sequences and groups the addresses. It also verifies postal discounts by tabulating mail counts in each Postal Code and Postal Walk. When the process is complete, all records will be in appropriate groups and sort order for efficient production, and all statistics required by CPC will be generated.

The processing through LCP software should not be confused with Address Accuracy and Correction. The former verifies only the postal code and the latter "triangulates" the postal code with the rest of the address. When a mailer wishes to mail 100% of the file for response analysis purposes, a pre-LCP should be performed to ensure that every record bears a valid postal code and passes the LCP approval process.

Customers should discuss data preparation issues with their direct mail services provider prior to sending out jobs. Making corrections to large data files and electronically transmitting them at the last minute may cause production problems. Even if high-speed data transmission is available, a five million record data file averaging 800 bytes per record still takes a long time to send and receive. In addition, your direct mailing services company still needs to get data to fit their format and more likely than not, some programming will be necessary. Although this usually isn't difficult, invariably time is limited this late in the production process.

PAL POINT... There's a lot to consider when planning your next direct mail job. With ever pending postal increases, it is more urgent than ever to squeeze out every cent of postal savings. Prevent production headaches by collaborating with your direct mail services provider early in the planning process. Working together, you should be able to develop a good data processing system that saves you time and money.

CHAPTER 17

Mailing Lists

There is little argument among direct mail experts that the mailing list constitutes the most vital component of a direct mail campaign. As attractive as an offer may be and as dynamic as the creative may look, these areas become inconsequential if the mailing is sent to the wrong audience.

The first step to consider when contemplating list selection is defining your target audience. Who are the most likely responders to the offer? If marketing to consumers, can you pinpoint certain demographics or psychographics (lifestyle characteristics) that seem to profile your likely customers? If you are a business-to-business marketer, do certain sized companies or industries make more sense than others? Are there geographic constraints? Ask yourself, "Where do my customers come from?" or, in the case of a new product or service, "What are the characteristics of my best prospects?"

Experienced mailing professionals know that analyzing core customer characteristics makes perfect sense. A formal way to accomplish this is to append customer and qualified prospect databases with business or consumer demographic data. There are less formal ways too, such as sending a brief survey to some of your best customers. In either case, it is important to understand as much as possible regarding your target audience because this will allow you to make intelligent list decisions, starting with the type of lists you purchase.

Two Classifications

The two general classifications of mailing lists are referred to as "compiled lists" and "response lists." Each is as it sounds. A compiled list is a grouping of common elements such as a list of all attorneys in a given area, for example. Compilers rely on public sources such as telephone books, directories, mortgage data, census data, annual reports and trade publications to gather as much data on individuals and businesses as possible. On the other hand, response lists are comprised of responders to direct mail, or other direct marketing solicitations. People and companies get placed on these lists because they buy, subscribe, attend, or donate.

All things equal, response lists typically outperform compiled lists since these names represent proven buyers of similar services or goods. Purchasers of compiled lists have no idea if any of the names are inclined at all to respond to direct mail solicitations; in fact, many will likely never respond. Not surprisingly, response lists are more expensive than compiled lists, but are usually justified because of their higher response rates. There are also unique selections, such as "recency" (newer names on lists are better prospects than those who purchased long ago but haven't since) and "price points" (some lists allow name selection based on the dollar volume of past purchases), both of which help bolster response rates but impractical for compiled lists.

Why bother with compiled lists? For starters, compiled lists are intended to provide as complete a universe of names as possible. Local merchants that cater to customers within a handful of Postal Codes would likely select compiled lists since a response list would likely yield very few names in a small geographic area. (Note: Many response lists have 5,000 name minimum order.) A business-to-business marketer looking to reach all CEOs with 100+ employees in a given state wouldn't want just those that subscribe to a particular publication. In cases like this, marketers would be better served by purchasing compiled lists.

Selection criteria for compiled lists are too numerous to discuss in depth. Some of the more popular parameters for business lists include:
• Industry (often via SIC codes)
• Employee count
• Sales volume
• Job title or function

There are also specialized files such as brand new businesses. Consumer selections include demographics such as:
- Age
- Estimated income
- Gender
- Presence of children
- Home ownership
- Length of residence
- Education level.

There are also many specialized databases offering everything from:
- New movers
- New homeowners
- People with home equity loans or second mortgages
- Pre- and postnatal women
- New businesses
- Sophisticated models based on various pieces of data designed to predict specific consumer behavior.

Finally, there are self-reported lists, often derived from questionnaires, surveys and product warranty cards. These lists rely on an individual completing information about themselves and their households and are regarded as being a bit more accurate than conventional compiled lists.

Once you're ready to embark upon list research, a good starting place is to contact the Canadian Marketing Association (CMA) at www.the-cma.org to find a list broker. List brokers should be willing to do a lot of legwork for you and recommend lists to suit your needs. Good brokers will also lend a hand in trafficking orders as well as in assisting with the tracking and monitoring of responses.

Mailers who are inclined to research lists on their own should acquaint themselves with list compilers and/or list managers. There are several major list compilers of consumer and business lists, many of which may be identified over the Internet.

Mailers that are interested in specific response or compiled lists can work directly with list managers, or have their brokers do so. The list manager, unlike a list broker, is the exclusive sales and marketing agent for specific list property. Many list management companies represent a lot of lists, many within the same category or subject area. Therefore, they may have additional list recommendations for you to consider. List managers are responsible for advertising and promoting their managed lists as well as fulfilling count requests, clearing sample mail pieces, coordinating orders with respective service bureaus, and collecting list rental revenues on the list owner's behalf.

PAL POINT... Choose your lists carefully! It's wise to end where we began. You can design the best possible piece and take advantage of all the postal discounts in the world, but if you mail to the wrong recipients, you'll waste a heck of a lot of your precious promotional budget.

Data Cleansing

Companies that manage your data, manage your future success. Fully service your data needs by selecting a data management services company with a wealth of direct mail industry knowledge. Experienced data partners will help you avoid pitfalls and costly errors while allowing you to get a good night's sleep. After verifying your instructions and requirements, a good data house will:

- Ensure your data files contain all required components, match the data file layout and are otherwise error-free.
- Build cleansing processes in a logical manner to ensure accurate data output.
- Extract a representative record dump to test the cleansing processes prior to full production. This will reduce the likelihood of logic errors and unnecessary multiple cleanup runs.
- Verify key fields such as Province codes. For example, "PQ" or "QU" are frequently used instead of the correct "QC."
- Check that apartment and suite numbers are located in a standardized position within an address field or are placed in a field of their own. Incorrect placement will reduce your project's chances for proper delivery.
- Ensure that proper recipient names are used. Up to 60% of the general population prefers to be addressed by a different salutation than the one used on most of their mail. Using a separate salutation field instead of a parsed first name field may boost your response rate. Properly place and punctuate name components such as honorific, first name, middle initial, last name, and suffix. Initial names like "J.R. Ewing" often are truncated to "Dear J."—unless a separate salutation field is used.
- Develop and update your house lists. Use a salutation field. Verify that each record has properly spelled name components (Claire, Clair, Clare), gender codes (Pat, Francis, Robin), casing (DeLane, Delane, deLane) and punctuation (L'Argent, Largent).

Merge/Purge

The de-duping process removes duplicate records from single or multiple data files. Before beginning merge/purge or any other type of data manipulation, it is critically important that you understand exactly what the client expects as output before giving instructions to your data processing department.

There are three levels of merge/purge for consumer files: resident, household, or individual. (Business-to-business lists require a different process.) Be sure to double check with your customer to determine what kind of list is being processed.

Resident level. This level of de-duplication removes all but one record from each address. For example, if John Doe and Mary Doe are each listed at 123 Main St. in separate records, only the first record will survive, while the other is dropped as a duplicate. The end result is that only one record will be mailed, which has an obvious associated cost saving.

Household level. This level removes all but one record with the same last name from each address. For example, if John Doe, Mary Doe, Sue Brown, and Joe Green all live at the same address, a household level de-duplication process will keep one of the Does, Sue Brown, and Joe Green. If John Doe appears in the data file first, Mary Doe will be dropped.

Individual level. This level will only remove duplicates with the same complete name from each address. For example if John Doe, Mary Doe, Sue Brown, and Joe Green all live at the same address, an individual de-duplication will keep ALL of the records since each one is a different person.

Additional Data Files

Suppression/purge. Often, clients request that certain people and/or households not receive mail. These types of requests, commonly referred to as "kill" files, can be made for many reasons. Two examples could be that they've been identified for nonpayment or poor payment or they've asked to be removed from your mailing list. In order to accommodate these types of requests, a customer-supplied "suppression" (a.k.a. "purge") file needs to be given. When records on the merge/purge file match records on the suppression file they're immediately dropped.

List priority. Some customers will furnish a "priority listing." This list will show which files take priority over other files when it comes to dropping duplicate records. This means that when duplicate records are found, the list with the highest priority loses the least amount of duplicate records because the duplicates are dropped from the lower priority files first. For example, if a customer supplies a "house" database file of customers as well as several rental files, the customer database will have the highest priority. The rental lists can then be ranked based upon rental costs. For example, assuming your most costly lists are more accurate, you'd probably want to assign a higher priority to the expensive lists and less priority to cheaper lists.

Before we go any farther, below are some terms that should be defined:

- **Duplicate elimination**—this process eliminates duplicates on one list, as defined by specified data logic on a job.
- **Merge/purge**—merge/purge is the elimination of "duplicates" as defined by the data logic on the specified project, across multiple lists. These lists are first merged together then duplicates are identified and subsequently purged from the output.
- **Match/merge**—the match/merge process first matches records, then merges similar ones together into one record. It is commonly used for financial or insurance companies needing to consolidate multiple accounts under the same name into one address.

Weighted-Value Merge/Purge

What happens when data files contain the same individual, but there's a misspelling? Would two pieces of mail be sent to John Doe and Jon Doe at the same address? If an individual merge/purge "match code" process were used, the answer would be "yes." (Match code merge/purges cannot compensate for key field character variation and will result in what is known as an "underkill.")

The solution to this vexing data problem is to perform a "weighted-value" merge/purge, whereby you determine which fields and record lengths are most appropriate for your project. Sophisticated weighted-value merge/purge algorithms enable you to avoid variances within name and address components and reduce your overkill/underkill error frequency. For example, a properly constructed weighted value merge/purge program will detect three variants of the following "Robert Tier" records and eliminate two:

1. Robert Tier,201 Carlaw Ave.,Toronto,ON,(416) 461-9271
2. Bob Tier,201 Carlaw Ave.,Toronto,ON,(416) 461-9201
3. Robert Teir,201 Carlaw Rd.,Toronto,ON,(416) 461-9271

Most merge/purges are based upon data files being sorted first by postal code in ascending sequence. Grouping records together by running an address verification/correction program prior to merge/purge is usually recommended. When multiple lists are used, a hierarchy (set of rules) should be created for the purpose of selecting the best data, thereby getting the most value out of the list. Here's an example for the following person, Mr. Jonathan Leopard, who prefers to be called "John":

- If a Salutation Field is present and populated, use "Dear <Salutation Field>" = "Dear John,"
- If no Salutation Field is present but First Name Field exists, use "Dear <First Name Field>" = "Dear Jonathan,"

- If First Name Field is not populated, use "Dear <Title> <Last Name>" = "Dear Mr. Leopard,"
- If no Title Field is available, use "Dear <Full Name>" = "Dear Jonathan Leopard,"

You can see that this progression starts "warm and personal" but moves by necessity toward "cool and formal," based on available data. Many service bureaus will help their clients make intelligent, informed decisions, but all involved in a project should be aware of what should be happening behind the scenes. Just be cognizant that the source data may be a limiting factor in the level of accuracy you can achieve in your quest for eliminating duplicates.

Address Accuracy/Address Correction (AA/AC)

Address Accuracy (and Correction) is a bit of a misnomer because it indicates that the addresses being processed are accurate, whereas they could be accurate but simply formatted contrary to CPC standards. Although an address may be "accurate" in our eyes and completely deliverable by Canada Post Corporation it may not be "accurate" when compared to the CPC database. The database is very specific as far as street types, abbreviations, and punctuation are concerned.

CPC-approved software will compare each address on a database and review it for a match against the CPC database. It will return a value of either accurate or inaccurate and a legend of the reasons for an inaccurate designation. Furthermore, the correction aspect of the software can then apply the changes to the output data. Finally, a

> **Tech Tip**
> Some clients may not wish for their data to be corrected or changed. For a file used multiple times throughout a year (such as a donor or subscription base), CPC allows Address Accuracy statements to be run once and retained on file for up to a year.

```
              *** StreetSweeper Address Accuracy Statement ***
    ==================================================================

      Run Date = Jul14/2005   File Name = BB_AUG05.DBF   Total Records = 448,058

      Valid      =  384,250     <Urban = 362,562>   <Rural =  21,688>
      Invalid    =   63,676     <Urban =  62,957>   <Rural =     719>
      Corrected  =   36,884     <Urban =  36,723>   <Rural =     161>

      Net Invalid =   26,792    <Urban =  26,234>   <Rural =     558>

    Total Canadian  447,926     <Urban = 425,519>   <Rural = 22,407>
               US       132
                    ========
    Grand Total     448,058
                              Errors  =      1
    ==================================================================
    Accuracy BEFORE Correction - Total  =  85.78%
                               - Urban  =  85.20%
                               - Rural  =  96.79%

      Accuracy AFTER  Correction - Total  =  94.02%
                               - Urban  =  93.83%
                               - Rural  =  97.51%
    ==================================================================
    StreetSweeper (tm) - Version 9 - Copyright Mailing Innovations


    ======================= << Correction Analysis >> ===============
    LV - Large Volume Receiver : 8       GK - GD Keyword            : 12
    LR - Apartment Building    : 7,301   DN - Delivery Name         : 27
    LB - Business Building     : 186     DI - Delivery Information   : 975
                                         MN - Municipal Name        : 7,328
    C# - Street (Civic) Number : 0       MA - Municipal Alternate   : 1,380
    SN - Street Name           : 8,684   AB - Municipal Abbreviation : 0
    ST - Street Type           : 8,644   PR - Province              : 3,303
    SD - Street Direction      : 4,540   PC - Postal Code           : 8,597
    SK - Suite Keyword         : 10,110  IP - Invalid Punctuation   : 1,204
    S# - Suite Number          : 7
    RK - Route Keyword         : 219
    R# - Route Number          : 346
    BK - PO Box Keyword        : 232
    B# - PO Box Number         : 0       Average Corrections/Address : 1.5
    ==================================================================
```

Sample address accuracy report. (Courtesy SMR•Tytrek)

report is produced showing accuracy levels before and after with a summary of issues and the number of records found relating to each issue on the database.

NCOA

The National Change of Address (NCOA) Service is the most accurate and up-to-date information available on recent movers in Canada. Each year, approximately 1.7 million individuals, families, and businesses move in Canada. Approximately 1.2 million of those movers file a Change of Address Notification (COAN) form with Canada Post Corporation when they move. This information is captured electronically and made available for those customers who have provided their consent to licensees of Canada Post's National Change of Address Data.

During use, a data file is matched against the "move" database. If a match is found, the new information is appended to the record. Only mailers can legally use this process; it cannot be used for any other purpose.

PAL POINT... Data cleansing is a vitally important activity and often makes a critical difference in terms of mailing deliverability, response rates, and profitability. For more detailed information on merge/purge, see Appendices 6 and 7.

Programming Issues

Programming is a generic term used to define various catchall functions related to preparing databases, formatting product layouts, creating tables and financial statements, completing customization and personalization of correspondence, and many other aspects of direct mail production. In our modern world of high technology, there is little that isn't touched in some way by programming. The capabilities are endless and the results are nothing short of miraculous.

Database Calculations

One of the most useful applications for programming involves combining database mailing lists with personalized information about likely purchasing preferences. There is a great value in knowing which prospects should receive what kinds of offers. For instance, financial institutions want to tailor their offers to meet the needs of specific clients and/or prospects. If a mailing within a particular neighborhood is going to target both established and new customers, the offers need to be significantly different to each target. Existing customers might be encouraged to refinance existing loans, or be enticed to take out new loans for luxury purchases. Other prospects might be offered attractive introductory rates based on their current credit scores. Another great value is the ability to track products and services a client may have previously purchased.

Output Formatting

The ability to tailor both information and offers to the specific needs of individual recipients means that special consideration needs to be paid to the physical aspects of each mailing. For example, the record for Mr. Alfaretto Manuel Joseph Constantinova, who is interested in four different magazines, is a lot longer than the one for John Smith with an interest in one magazine. The person designing a mailing containing both records has to make sure that the mailing design can accommodate the physical requirements of both, especially if a variable image is to be attached to each magazine code. If the only concern is for addressing, it is possible to fill the space with both names by increasing or reducing the font sizes for that line. An alternative for data lines that are too long is to abbreviate some common words such as Boulevard, Terrace, Street, Avenue, and Parkway.

Let's turn our attention to a consumer's previous purchasing behavior. Perhaps Alfaretto has used Joe's Garage for oil changes in the past. During Al's last visit, the proprietor Joe recorded that Al's tires and brake pads are wearing a little thin and might be receptive to a deal on those items during his next oil change. Since Al is like most people and needs an oil change every three months, Joe writes an appropriate note in his database. Joe wants to increase his market share and outperform the competition. One month before Al's expected return, he receives his reminder to schedule his oil change, which also has attractive offers on a new set of tires and brake pads, but only if he pre-schedules his visit on a Thursday, which is Joe's typically slow day. Not surprisingly, Joe's mailing services programmer is very competent and notices that this highly personalized communication to Al is too long and will wrap onto a second page, which inconveniently doesn't exist. But since this problem was anticipated during the design of this direct mail program, programming code was written to automatically alter the text size and image layout.

There are an infinite number of possible variations, most of which can be achieved by efficient—and in some cases downright clever—programming. The ability to anticipate obstacles and program workaround solutions adds value to the products and services that direct mailers offer. This is

what helps drive up response rates, revenue, and profit—all
of which build customer loyalty.

Consider the Costs

Limit costs by sanitizing your database during the planning
stages of a mailing campaign. For instance, if a detailed database is submitted by the client that employs all of the proper
notations, has been efficiently parsed, and is correctly labeled
and delineated, then the upfront cost should be lower. On the
contrary, if the list is segmented, poorly labeled or possibly
out of date, the programmer will require a greater number
of hours to prepare that list.

The cost of database pro-
gramming is typically billed
by the hour. The process
can involve two steps: first,
preparing the list, and
second, programming the
data fields; where each
name or detail from the
list is inserted.

Lists come in several formats, the most common of
which are .dbf files, text-
based files and, to a lesser
degree, Excel spreadsheets. Text files must be properly
delimited, meaning each field item (prefix, name, street
address, city and province, postal code, suffix) must be set
apart in the database file by a comma, tab, colon, or space.
Use a single line for each entry, a line break indicates a new
record. Follow these guidelines so the file can easily be
imported into MS Excel. Using a column for each field in an
MS Excel file automatically accomplishes the same tasks.
Include column headers. This is important when a one-up
piece has variable content.

Tech Tip: For a print program to accurately insert names and addresses in the correct fields, the database must be properly formatted. Direct mail houses can prepare the list, however, hourly fees apply. Save money by properly formatting the lists prior to submission.

It has become commonplace for a direct mail piece to have a totally customized design, including images, language, and special offers. These features are additional fields that must be included in the database and the programming framework, which drives up the labor cost. Remember the example of Joe's Garage? Total customization can reap huge benefits for large and small businesses. The response will likely outweigh the expense.

If the product is to be designed to pull variable images, languages, and offers to be switched up based on the recipient, then the programmer will have to dedicate a great deal of time to the variable sets. If X requires Y and Y requires Z and YZ requires D to effectively output G, then the programmer will be required to dedicate a great deal of time to setting these strings in place to run accurately and efficiently—these and every combination therein. Time is money and programmers don't come cheaply. With effective preplanning, the costs can be minimized. However, in most cases programming times are approximations that need to be clearly communicated to customers. Plan ahead for these costs and relate to customers that the programming hours involved may be greater or smaller depending on the issues encountered.

PAL POINT... Intelligent use of programming helps direct mailers be more personal and effective. The results of spelling mistakes, wrong offers or badly tailored information can be devastating. Don't take output for granted: Test all variables to make sure that you're using your available data in the best possible way. Does the end result work the way it should? Does it read properly and look the way it should? Programming errors can easily change a recipient's mind from "YES, I'll buy because this speaks to me," to "NO, I won't buy because you don't know me and obviously don't care."

File Transportation

Efficient transportation of electronic data between people and companies is very important in today's fast-paced business environment. Over the past two decades, data transportation has evolved from slow and bulky mediums such as magnetic tapes, disks, and cartridges (still in use by some list brokers and utility companies because of database size and complexity) to CDs and other optical media to completely electronic transmission, which doesn't require physical transportation of any sort.

Data Security

File formats and transmission methods can have a dramatic impact on both the quality and speed of mail production. With the advent of highly publicized identity theft and other data-related crimes, security during the data transportation process is becoming a much more important issue with each passing month.

Many financial companies have moved toward sophisticated data encryption techniques. By converting confidential data into encrypted formats, valuable private information can be transmitted and shared much more safely among users with a need to know. Even when prying eyes intercept encrypted files, they are useless without the ability to decode the data. More companies, even those well outside the financial services arena, are rapidly moving toward this kind of protection as the concern for privacy and identity theft continues to rise.

At first glance, the encryption and subsequent decryption of data appears to be another cumbersome step in the direct mail process, sometimes perceived as being unnecessary. However, it is important to protect all databases and is the responsibility of all responsible mailers and their service providers. If the direct mail community is not diligent about protecting direct marketing's biggest asset, our industry eventually will be legislated, likely with negative consequences. The authors firmly believe it is better to be proactive, responsible, and ahead of the curve where security is concerned.

For most direct mail applications, a common method of moving data from one point to another is electronic file transfer. Although regular email allows people to conveniently transfer files of moderate size, this popular method is not nearly as secure or reliable as some other electronic file transfer options. Email can get hung up in a variety of ways. For example, most email servers have size restrictions that can prevent successful transmission. On the recipient's end, spam filters that aren't properly set to accept a new address can also hold up production as people struggle to find out where the recently sent data temporarily resides. The bottom line is this: when programmers have to wait for email to arrive or must play phone tag when it doesn't, production is slowed and deadlines are threatened.

FTP File Transfer

The most efficient and reliable way to move files without a physical medium is file transfer protocol (FTP). Any server can be configured using secure, password-protected folders where a client may deliver or retrieve large amounts of data or image files. There are many FTP tools available that make it easy to select, upload, and download files directly to a server. Rights to distribute these tools are often free and can be supplied to customers. FTP greatly simplifies the production process and enhances the security of the transaction.

PAL POINT... There have been many advancements in our ability to safely and quickly send large amounts data from anywhere to anywhere. As the need for privacy and security continues to rise in importance, progressive direct mailers must continually invest in these tools to comply with rapidly changing market demands.

Building Data Tables

Here's an attractive goal: *reduce data entry and computing processing time while increasing accuracy.* How? Build "tables" into your database.

One of the authors' friends in the direct mail industry had a china manufacturing client. If his data entry staff was required to type "bone white," "forest green," or "Antarctica White," into the colour field, you can be certain that there would be many misspellings. If specific offers for more china were dependent on getting the colour right, wouldn't it be more efficient to assign a number to this particular field in each record? Of course it would.

Typing a number such as "03" or a short string of letters such as "ant" instead of "Antarctica White" is a lot faster and far less subject to data entry errors. Then, when your mailing house processes the mail, the field entry would be cross-referenced to the data table with the china patterns and "Antarctica White" would be properly printed in the body of the letter. Better yet, more tables can be created that suggest other Antarctica White coloured products, which will help cross-sell and up-sell existing customers.

Now consider the automobile industry. Most manufacturers periodically send different promotional offers to their customers based on demographic information contained in various tables. Some of these companies believe in local control and subsequently push

TECH TIP

In addition, data tables reduce computer-processing time because each record contains fewer bytes. Although today's computing technology has vastly improved, smaller files still mean faster data processing and transmission times. This is especially true if limited bandwidth data communications lines are involved.

many marketing decisions down the decision chain as far as the dealer level. Participating dealers are able to choose which promotions to offer, such as $20 off a lube job, free wipers, car wash, etc. In addition to being variable (i.e., discount amount), these offers are referenced in different tables so dealers can easily choose multiple promotions if they wish. If so, all they have to do is say to their direct mail services company, "For our next mailing, we want promos 1, 4, 8, and 13 mailed sequentially to our database." And that is exactly what they'd get. (See chapter 22, "Nth Criteria Select.")

Organizations that input a lot of data should consider creating and using templates that restrict data entry to what can be considered as valid data for that field. This might be as simple as having only the alphanumeric codes that are valid as a set of acceptable input key strokes. If a data entry clerk enters a string of key strokes that do not match one of the strings on the list, the template will not accept the data until it's corrected. There are software programs that will verify that an address exists within Canada as the data is being entered. This is a great tool for verifying data at the source, thereby reducing the amount of data integrity issues further down the production process.

PAL POINT... The use of shortened numbers makes life easy. For example, look at what McDonald's has done to simplify the meal ordering process. No longer do you have to give a laundry list of items: Just say, "number two, please." McDonald's has wisely discovered that ordering by number reduces ambiguity and human error, while being more efficient. As a bonus, product bundling increases the average order size.

Nth Criteria Select

What happens when you wish to send a mailing to only a portion of your database? There are many reasons why you may need to do this. Budgeting, test marketing, and target marketing all come to mind.

Let's say you have 100,000 mailing records in your database and for budget reasons can only afford to send 80,000 pieces. In this case, don't send mail to the first 80,000 people and skip the rest. Doing so may result in your skipping all records in California for instance, which would badly skew the results. A better way to proceed would be to select eight out of every ten records—in this case, sequentially by Postal Code—via an "Nth criteria select" process. If your mailing house deselects every fifth and tenth record, your mailing size will end up at the desired 80,000 pieces and each Postal Code will be proportionately reduced.

Nth criteria select needn't only be done by geography. Perhaps you're working on a high-cost/high-profile piece that targets large charitable donors. Due to this project's parameters, you will need your average donation size to be larger than usual to justify the cost of the promotion. It may make sense to target people and organizations with histories of donating large amounts in the past. If so, go into your field with previous donation historical data and select only those records that meet or exceed a certain threshold of giving.

Nth Criteria Select Examples

Example 1. Once again consider the company that manufactures fine china. Whenever certain china patterns are due to go on sale, they query the database to identify household in that have bought the same patterns in the past and send a highly targeted mailing just to those people. Also, this same company regularly tries to give a few stores at a time a sales

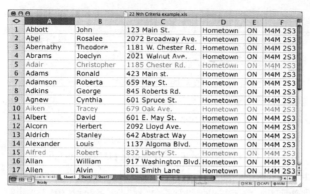

	A	B	C	D	E	F
1	Abbott	John	123 Main St.	Hometown	ON	M4M 2S3
2	Abel	Rosalee	2072 Broadway Ave.	Hometown	ON	M4M 2S3
3	Abernathy	Theodore	1181 W. Chester Rd.	Hometown	ON	M4M 2S3
4	Abrams	Joeclyn	2021 Walnut Ave.	Hometown	ON	M4M 2S3
5	Adair	Christopher	1185 Chester Rd.	Hometown	ON	M4M 2S3
6	Adams	Ronald	423 Main st.	Hometown	ON	M4M 2S3
7	Adamson	Roberta	659 May St.	Hometown	ON	M4M 2S3
8	Adkins	George	845 Roberts Rd.	Hometown	ON	M4M 2S3
9	Agnew	Cynthia	601 Spruce St.	Hometown	ON	M4M 2S3
10	Aiken	Tracey	679 Oak Ave.	Hometown	ON	M4M 2S3
11	Albert	David	601 E. May St.	Hometown	ON	M4M 2S3
12	Alcorn	Herbert	2092 Lloyd Ave.	Hometown	ON	M4M 2S3
13	Aldrich	Stanley	642 Abstract Way	Hometown	ON	M4M 2S3
14	Alexander	Louis	1137 Algoma Blvd.	Hometown	ON	M4M 2S3
15	Alfred	Robert	832 Liberty St.	Hometown	ON	M4M 2S3
16	Allan	William	917 Washington Blvd.	Hometown	ON	M4M 2S3
17	Allen	Alvin	801 Smith Lane	Hometown	ON	M4M 2S3

An example of a database in which every fifth name is selected.

boost by sending promotional mailings to people who have shopped in these stores before. However, they have rigid spending guidelines and use an Nth criteria select process to mail to get their costs exactly in line.

Example 2. The financial community sends out many promotional mailings. Nth criteria select methods allow clients to choose recipients based on desired credit scores and make different offers to different people based on credit worthiness. For example, your good credit may get you a pre-approved credit card with a low rate while your next-door neighbor may get an offer for a secured card at 21% interest. If you don't like the way this sounds, this is absolutely an everyday occurrence.

PAL POINT... Like so much else in direct mail, it's the little things that count. The Nth criteria select process helps mailing professionals meet their budget constraints while properly targeting their best prospects.

Address Standards

There are innumerable ways that mailings can go awry. In order to comply with CPC rules and achieve maximum postal discounts, many rules need to be followed. CPC demands the highest level of address accuracy and will assess penalties when not respected.

Statement of Accuracy (SOA)

Customers that use Incentive Lettermail, Addressed Admail, Publications Mail, and/or Dimensional Admail must meet the Address Accuracy Program requirements. A 95% accuracy rate is mandated for all database mailings. To avoid a penalty, a Statement of Accuracy (SOA) is required to verify the

```
            *** Canada Post Address Accuracy Statement ***
            ==================================================

SOFTWARE COMPANY NAME:

        Mailing Innovations
        20-3397 American Drive
        Mississauga On   L4V 1T8
        Canada

SOFTWARE VERSION:

        StreetSweeper - Version 9 (CPC Recognized - Sept 30, 2005)

CANADA POST ADDRESS TAPE DATE:

        JULY 1 TO SEPTEMBER 15

CUSTOMER NAME:

        The SMR Group
        201 Carlaw Ave
        Suite 200
==================================================================================

TOTAL NUMBER OF RECORDS PROCESSED:

        Total = 448,058

VALIDATION/CORRECTION DATE:

        Jul14/2005

ADDRESS ACCURACY LEVEL (CANADA POST STANDARD RATING):

                        =====>   94.02%   <=====
==================================================================================

FILE NAME:    J:\WORK\19124\DAT\BB_AUG05.DBF




Signature: _____    Date: _____
```

Sample address accuracy statement. (Courtesy SMR•Tytrek)

Start 2 bars	DCI 3 bars	Postal Code 12 bars	Address Locator 21 bars	PT 5 bars	Customer Information 25 bars	RS Parity 12 bars	Stop 2 bars

L3B 4T9   142A _ _ _ _ _   123456789012345

Components of a postal barcode.

percentage of accurate addresses on a mailing list. Customers must keep a valid copy of the SOA on file in the event that Canada Post requests a copy. The lists must be regularly processed and synchronized with the CPC database. Anything less than 95% accuracy will be assessed a penalty. Process the database through Canada Post-recognized Address Validation or Address Validation and Correction software or by using a mail service provider that offers this service. Only Software Evaluation and Recognition Program (SERP) approved programs are deemed true and accurate. Before taking chances, confirm that the mail house contracted uses this standard.

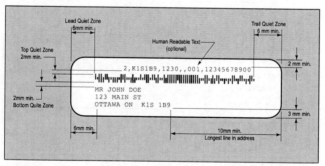

Standards for positioning of an address in an envelope window.

PAL POINT... Automation reduces costs and increases financial rates of return. While there are investments involved with adding new equipment and software, the overall long-term savings in sorting and preparation can make a measurable difference in the bottom line.

PDF Workflow

24

Both the printing and direct mail industries continue to evolve from the arcane method of stripping film. New technologies that turn electronic art files into beautifully printed pieces are improving almost daily, or so it seems. But with greater features comes greater complexity. How do you keep up with the changes? Well, the answer can be found in just three letters: PDF.

PDF, or Portable Document Format, is almost everywhere. Perhaps you've downloaded PDF files as a convenient way to print anything from maps, tax forms, and instruction sheets. Well, PDF technology works wonders in ink-on-paper environments as well. PDFs are an essential part of a digital workflow system that gets jobs out quickly, accurately and with greater flexibility.

The accuracy of a PDF file is unparalleled, since every aspect of a document to be printed is included in the file—most importantly, images and fonts. In a properly created PDF, the fonts are actually written into the file's code. There's no more hunting for fonts or seeing the wrong font make its way onto a proof! With a PDF-based workflow, a lot of time-consuming prepress tasks are eliminated.

Online Proofing

The capabilities of the PDF format as a proofing method are nearly limitless. Again, there simply is no comparison between a PDF-based proofing system and most traditional proofing methods in terms of speed. In some cases,

> **Tech Tip**
>
> The key to the flexibility of a PDF workflow is that a single PDF file contains all the information necessary to see a job through its entire life cycle, not just during the printing process itself. The same file that's used to create the printed piece can be viewed online as a proof.

"proofing" used to mean actually printing a sample piece for the client, right on a press. Sure, it looked great, but it took forever to do. And changes? These could tack hours onto the job.

The PDF workflow system improves on the past tremendously by allowing proofing to be done online, in full colour on a computer monitor. The same file that will actually be used to print the job is available via email or on the Web as soon as it's ready for proofing. This "instant access" shaves off a great deal of valuable time for direct mailers either printing or outsourcing project components, because it allows them to immediately make changes to the proof.

Another key benefit to viewing proofs online is that multiple parties can see the same file simultaneously. If two decision makers can't be in the same office, building, or even the same area code, they can both view and make changes to the PDF file. Currently, this is accomplished via email. However, there soon should be an interface that will allow several users to collaborate at a single Website, making changes in real time and seeing those changes immediately noted in the image onscreen.

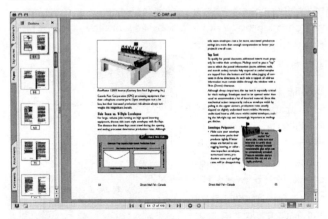

A PDF of the Direct Mail Pal—Canada *being viewed online, in this case for author approval.*

Don't mistake online PDF proofs as just a "quick and dirty" tool for monitoring the progress of a job. Many project managers appreciate the efficiency of PDF proofs so much that they make final approvals based on them. Though the colour onscreen is not exactly as it will appear on the printed piece, many direct mail services clients feel it is close enough and therefore don't require an actual hardcopy colour proof, unless it's a colour-critical job. Of course, a good rapport between direct mailer and client is essential for PDF proofs to be the sole proofing method.

PAL POINT... Although implementing PDF-based job and inventory management systems can appear complex, trust your comprehensive direct mail services provider to guide the process of developing a faster and more accurate workflow.

100% Mailings

There are occasions when a mailing services client needs all addresses on their database to be sent mail…guaranteed. If your job involves invoices, account statements, proxies, annual reports, etc., you need 100% deliverability. This is in contrast to many promotional mailings where some spoilage is acceptable. If you've been through this process before, you probably understand some of the basic complexities of what is known in the industry as "100% mailings." The rule of thumb when producing 100% mailings is to plan for this requirement at the beginning of a job.

To comply, your mailing services company must alter its standard operating procedures to maneuver around an unavoidable manufacturing reality: production spoilage. Manufacturing processes must be implemented that ensure the recapture of all pieces spoiled during production. Then, these pieces need to be identified, matched against the master database, and produced again in a follow-up production run.

Some mailers advise customers with 100% mailing requirements to design an area somewhere on their piece where a unique barcode can be imaged. After the first production run, they gather all spoilage and scan every piece, giving an electronic record locator that shows which addresses need to be recreated. Next, the scanned results are downloaded and matched against the original database

TECH TIP

By far the least efficient method of data recapture is manually re-keying printed data—which usually involves filling in the name and address fields. Once completed, a match against the original database is run. Since so many more keystrokes are required by this tedious method, job turnaround time increases, as does the frequency of data entry errors.

to create a new data file. Then, the previously spoiled pieces are run twice (just in case the rerun is spoiled too) are re-imaged, thereby producing a new mailing that plugs the gaps of the first, returning the desired result: A 100% mailing.

In the event that your client won't allow you to image a bar-code anywhere on the piece, the process of matching spoilage to the master database becomes more time-consuming. When barcodes are objectionable, try to convince the decision maker to at least let you print a unique sequence number (a type of record locater) inconspicuously placed somewhere on the piece. If you can, data file recreation only involves the additional step of rekeying a short string of text characters from each spoiled piece, enabling the computer to identify the addresses for reimaging. While rekeying sequence numbers is less efficient and precise than barcode scanning, it sure beats the last alternative: manual rekeying of field data.

In general, plan to add an additional 10% to the cost of production, more or less depending on project complexity and the number of manufacturing operations involved. If the project is straightforward, such as laser imaging, converting, and inserting, your mailing services provider should antici-pate minimal spoilage and your price premium should be somewhere near 10%. However, if your job involves a lot of additional bindery or other manufacturing operations, there will be more spoilage and this premium percentage will increase, perhaps to 20%.

PAL POINT... 100% mailings require extra planning, mate-rials, machine makereadies, and production time. It should be no surprise that 100% mailings cost more to produce.

Self-Mailer Programs

On any given day, take a look at the promotional mail in your mailbox. How much of it consists of materials stuffed in envelopes? How many "self-mailers" did you receive? Why should self-mailers care about this ratio? Simply put: cost vs. benefit.

In general, self-mailers require fewer manufacturing production steps than mailings requiring traditional folding and envelope insertion. Fewer manufacturing steps results in lower costs and is attractive for this reason, among others. For definition purposes, anytime a piece is designed with the return address, address, and postage on the piece itself, rather than being stuffed into an envelope, it can be called a self-mailer.

This simple concept goes beyond the idea of a postcard. Creative use of folding, scoring and perforating techniques, permanent (seam) glue, remoistenable glue, diecutting, inkjet imaging, and tab and wafer seals allows the direct mail project designer to boost response rates while holding costs down.

Unique Ideas

Properly designed self-mailers can accomplish most of what envelopes do and more. Would you like your mailing to contain a CD, DVD, magnet, small calendars, coin, or a key? With increasingly available attaching technology, you can! For example, when Chrysler introduced the PT Cruiser in North America, dealers in several markets mailed a key in a folded self-mailer to carefully selected recipients. The promotion was this: bring the mailed key into the dealership, and if the key started the car, the lucky winner got to drive it home.

For talented creative directors, the self-mailer promotional category offers unique opportunities for generating both revenue and profits. Zipper perforations, moving pieces, pop-ups, diecuts, intrigue-generating folding sequences, glued

Promotional CDs. (Courtesy SMR•Tytrek)

attachments, encapsulated loose inserts, perforated BRCs, gusseted pockets, and many more self-mail design capabilities are all possible. Self-mailers can include stitched or spine-pasted components, personalized products, introductory samples, or geographically targeted maps. As long as you have access to a competent direct mail services provider, stretch your creativity…you just might be surprised at what's possible.

Variations in design offer a change of pace for the consumer. By engaging the recipient with out-of-the-ordinary promotional concepts, creative marketers earn more time and attention, thus increasing the odds of generating a favorable response.

Self-mailers can accommodate the design needs of both bargain basement and Rolex-type products, and many things in between. Not surprisingly, the use of self-mailers is steadily growing. Frequently self-mailer projects are born from necessity. It is up to the production partner to identify specific needs and suggest appropriate project designs. As already implied, these processes could include traditional lettershop and bindery services to specialty finishing, diecutting, attaching, gluing, and more. Don't be afraid to reach out and be unique.

Sourcing Direct Mail Production

The more complex a self-mailer, the more time should be allocated for production. Although some inline web production processes exist that can create attractive self-mailer designs, the majority of the ones that truly stand out typically require multiple processes. There are two typical ways of tackling complex self-mailer production.

The first is for the client to coordinate all multiple processes involved. This means that they sub out the printing, bindery, finishing, and mailing processes. For complex jobs, a half-dozen or more vendors may be involved. This approach could look good on paper because a few pennies may be saved.

The second approach is to choose a lead production partner who is willing to take on the entire job by either completing all or most of the processes in house and outsource the

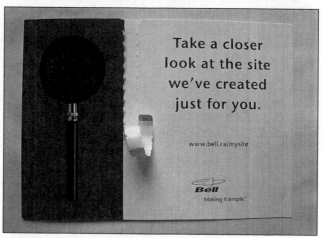

Unique self-mailer design including zipper perforations, tipped-on magnifying glass, and web decoder. (Courtesy Innovative Graphics)

rest. This approach may cost a few pennies more, because project coordination is a valuable service and requires compensation. However, the biggest benefit with this approach is accountability. Your lead production partner should assume all coordination responsibilities, which in turn should free you up to concentrate on what you do best.

Be conscious of every step required before moving a piece from one vendor to another. It is important to include production partners early in the planning process. The project should be walked through step by step with the person responsible for each step making comments and committing to what they can and cannot do. Once agreed, the concept can be turned into reality.

PAL POINT... What may seem like a great idea may turn out to be impractical in production or too expensive to produce. During the design stage, carefully consider the end-user experience. The point of a self-mailer is to be unique and cost-effective. Don't defeat the purpose.

Postcard Programs

If you're looking for a proven, low cost direct response marketing vehicle, consider the timeless, versatile...and yes, safe...postcard. Compared to other types of printed promotions, postcard campaigns are relatively inexpensive to produce. They deserve extra consideration, especially when timeliness and cost considerations are paramount.

Production and Postal Issues

There are a few critical design issues that should be considered when developing postcard mailings.

- **Size.** To qualify for postcard rates, pieces must be between 235×120 mm and 140×90 mm. Anything larger will mail at letter-size mail rates.

- **Paper thickness.** Most designers know that 7-pt. high bulk is the minimum postcard thickness. However, even though this weight of paper meets CPC standards, it often has a flimsy feel to it. Consider increasing your paper thickness to 9-pt. or even higher. CPC standards measure 0.18 mm to 5 mm and must be below 50 grams in weight.

- **Double postcards.** Folded postcards with perforated BRCs qualify for postcard postal rates, if the attached card is a true BRC. This means the second panel of the card must be detachable and mailable as a reply device. Don't add a folded panel just because you're running out of visual real estate. Otherwise, you'll end up with a rude postage surprise. The address side of the reply card must be folded inward. Also, the two panels must be sealed with one seal at either the top or the bottom.

- **Multiple versions.** If you're planning a multi-postcard campaign or printing similar versions together, specifying all the jobs to run together could save both time and money. Ganged production runs are just one area for potential savings. Also consider plate changes for simple text differences.

Postcard Design: A Case Study

A friend of one the authors recently changed his company's phone system. As a result, hundreds of her employees were assigned new direct dial extensions. Word of this change had to be communicated to customers and vendors quickly. Direct mail, broadcast fax, broadcast email, and word of mouth through the sales and customer service teams were considered. This company's marketing department felt that a postcard mailing targeted to all customers, vendors, and industry friends would be the best channel to reach everyone as quickly and directly as possible.

Deb Tompkins, sales manager for JAM Communications, one of the project advisors, provided the following insights:

> *"Postcards can solve company-specific marketing problems. Don't struggle with the endless search for the 'perfect' image, because it rarely exists. Instead, consider creating original artwork. Since the physical aspects of postcards are limited, they cry out for creative, jazzy, and unusual designs. Get my attention with the artwork. Then keep the copy brief and simple, but personalize it whenever possible."*

PAL POINT... If you're looking for a different way to get your message to your marketplace, or if you have budget constraints, consider a postcard program. Postcards aren't just for vacation pictures anymore.

28

Personalized Labels

Labels are a great way for both nonprofit organizations and for-profit companies to achieve great direct mail results. Many direct mailers have pigeonholed label programs as effective, but infrequent seasonal events. There are two problems with this approach. First, direct mailers are missing out on good opportunities with a proven marketing vehicle. Second, program managers don't learn how to efficiently purchase and administer them.

There are a lot of companies and organizations that only think of direct mail label programs for the winter holiday season. This is outdated thinking. Many label jobs now have mail drop dates in the late winter, spring, and summer. Labels aren't just for the holiday season anymore.

Mailing professionals who buy a lot of the same direct mail components become skilled at squeezing good results out of small investments. However, infrequent purchases don't attract the same scrutiny as other programs and tend not to be bought as efficiently. Opting for the "easy" purchase route may cost you more than you realize. Let's examine why labels are effective as promotional items.

Labels Work

Today's specialty landscape is full of promotional products. Direct mail label programs have endured because recipients get a useful product that can be used every day and proudly displays their affinity with a desirable organization. As a result, the target audience is likely to respond favorably to the solicitation request. Historically, nonprofit organizations have been the main users of label programs because their target audiences appreciate the functionality of the labels themselves and are eager to display their affinity with the soliciting organization.

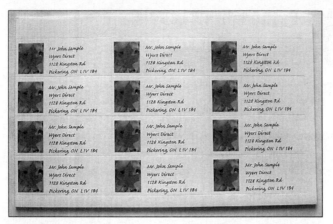

Sample personalized mailing labels. (Courtesy Wyers Direct)

Labels are desirable premiums because (1) production can be highly automated and (2) final product can be easily delivered through CPC. Many competing specialty products such as pens, small calendars, and coffee cups can't be manufactured as easily and cost more to mail without necessarily producing better response rates. Sheets of labels can be designed as just another insert in a direct mail package. Since they are so automation-friendly, labels are very appropriate for high-volume mailings.

Labels Work in the For-Profit Arena Too

Although nonprofits have been the traditional users of direct mail label programs, for-profit companies have discovered ways of hopping on the bandwagon. For example, some financial institutions advise their customers to attach labels imprinted with theft protection information to their credit cards before initial use. If a consumer's cards have "protection" labels affixed to them and are stolen, the theory is that thieves will be deterred from using them. Non-financial-sector companies have sent labels to their customers for use on windshields, phones, and membership cards. Labels are an inexpensive way to disburse useful information in bite-sized doses.

Design Flexibility

Direct mail labels can follow traditional formats, or may be designed to be as unique as fingerprints. The following features can be added or changed to meet your special marketing needs:

- Size of the sheet
- Number of ink colours
- Foil stamping
- Size and position of folds and panels
- Label paper stock and colour
- Intricate diecuts
- Label size and shape
- Number of labels per sheet and per recipient
- Graphics
- Sheet orientation (landscape/portrait)

Design options are unlimited. When designing your label sheet, allow $\frac{1}{2}$ in. (13 mm) margin for pin feed holes on each side of the paper. Some label manufacturers can print, foil-stamp, diecut, and strip away waste inline before imprinting, inserting, and drop shipping or mailing. If you're straying from standard label formats, get advice early in the design process because some designs can't have waste automatically stripped, which dramatically increases costs.

Tech Tip

Don't forget about mailing discounts. Since labels can be inserted just like any other mailing component, you can benefit from most postal savings programs.

Buying Expertise

Direct mail professionals have a lot of options when purchasing label programs. As mentioned earlier, most people do not buy label programs often and this may result in comparatively low levels of buying expertise. Outsourcing direct mail label programs to "professional fundraising companies" is attractive to some people because it is easy. In exchange for a healthy portion of the net proceeds, a professional fundraising company will handle the entire program for a client, soup to nuts. Essentially, all a nonprofit administrator has to do is handoff a mailing list, wait a few months and receive a check for a portion of the funds raised.

However, if a nonprofit wishes to maximize net revenue, it should consider buying the label program direct. In exchange for a little more hands-on management, a nonprofit can significantly increase its fundraising net revenues. For example, if a label program costs $50,000 to produce and administer, and generates $100,000 of funds, the contribution margin is $50,000. If a professional fundraiser is involved, this $50,000 will be split somehow between the fundraising company and the nonprofit. Professional management companies may not take advantage of the latest manufacturing technology and since the client has little direct involvement, production and administrative costs tend to be very high. A scenario in which the nonprofit receives less than half of the normal net proceeds (in this case, $25,000) is certainly possible.

Label program managers in this situation should ask the question: "Does the ease of working with a professional fundraiser offset the loss of $25,000?" Some will answer, "yes" and others, "no," depending on their circumstances.

PAL POINT... Label programs work because they shout, "I'm a member." This is good for both the label giver and the end user because they enter a symbiotic relationship whereby both parties benefit. Encourage your customers to buy direct mail label programs smarter and more frequently.

3 Direct Mail Production

29

Letter Text and Variable Imaging

One of the certainties of the direct mail industry is that the pace will keep on quickening. Even though mailings are more complex than ever, turnaround times nonetheless are becoming shorter. From a copywriter and designer's point of view, waiting until the last minute has a benefit because the latest and most relevant information can be added. However, delay has negative consequences that ripple throughout the production process.

Let's consider how compressed schedules affect letter text and variable image positioning. In the not too distance past, simple text files were converted into laser formats that were limited at best, which easily allowed text to be "dropped in" at the last moment. Even though today's sophisticated "publishing" tools have made incredible gains in the world of personalization, on the data preparation side, there are now more ways than ever for something to go wrong. The bottom line is this: Try to give your mailing services provider enough time so they can confidently prepare your job and meet your scheduling needs.

Expectations

At a minimum, data preparation and mail service providers should be able to accept text formatted as word processing documents, thereby retaining most properties intended by the designer and marketer. Even better is if graphic layout program files, such as QuarkXPress and Adobe's InDesign, can be accepted. If so, the actual designer's file can be used, complete with variable and static text and graphic images.

When your direct mail service provider laser-images your variable copy on either cut-sheet or continuous forms, there are many things they must be aware of to prevent costly production errors.

Matt Copy

When a personalized letter, reply, or document is part of the job, make sure decision makers see and approve a "matt copy," which is the part of the letter, reply, or document that will be "pre-printed" prior to shipping the form to your mail services provider for customization. This helps ensure that personalization, variable laser imaging, and preprinting all match in typeface, size and style.

Tech Tip: It's best if clients provide this "matt copy" in electronic form in an acceptable format. Once the mailing services provider's data processing department has set the matt copy, the "proof" should be read for typographical, spelling, punctuation, spacing, and any other kinds of errors.

Whitepaper Proofs

Prior to live laser sign-offs, "whitepaper" proofs (laser-imaged proofs on plain paper) should be created so only that which is to be laser-imaged is clearly seen. Again, as with matt copy the entire document must be proofed, word for word, graphic by graphic. Look for items such as:

- Spacing between words
- Spacing between lines
- Placement of name & address block
- Codes (check number of digits, alphanumeric, starting digit, etc.)

Be certain that the approved matt copy and the laser-printed text and images agree.

Live Laser Proofs

Once the whitepaper sign-offs have been approved and all data file processing is complete, the mailing services company should offer "live" laser sign-offs for final approval. Again, verify accuracy of copy, text, and window positioning before

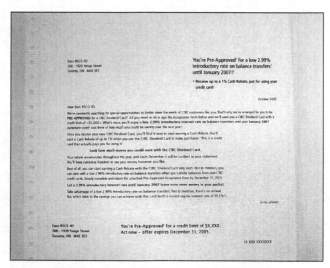

Sample of whitepaper proof. (Courtesy Euro RSCG 4D)

beginning the production run. Both the client and the account manager must verify the proof for accuracy.

Lastly, be wary of pushing the variable personalization envelope beyond the integrity of your data. For example, sending a personalized solicitation expounding benefits of a female health club to a male named "Pat" will be ineffective at best and more likely will do more harm than good.

PAL POINT... Do not rush through the seemingly tedious proofing process. Find a quiet spot, go through the file, concentrate on that specific job, and then begin proofing. Take your time, because this is where a lot of mistakes happen. Try not to compress turnaround times beyond the turnaround guidelines preferred by your direct mail services provider. Although it may be possible to occasionally shorten delivery dates, the chances of error do increase.

Levels of Personalization

Personalization can range from a name and address block to a handwritten letter, to anything in between. Due to superior speed and quality, laser imaging is still a very popular method of addressing and personalizing direct mail forms. Over the last decade, technological improvements in inkjet imaging have enabled the direct mail industry to leap forward in terms of personalization capabilities.

Variable Inkjet Imaging

There are various levels of personalization. The most common form of personalization is a name and address block used on most Addressed Admail and Lettermail pieces. In direct mail's infancy, name and address were applied to a mail piece by way of a computer-generated label called a Cheshire label. Today, inkjet technology has all but replaced these labels.

Next on the scale of personalization is the addition of a salutation line. This has become quite common on many mail pieces in an effort to appeal to each individual. A salutation line is formatted as a common letter with "Dear" and then the individual's name. Although it is appealing to use a person's name in a salutation line, marketers should be cautious as it relates to their market, product, and the list(s) they are using. For business products and even many financial products, the more formal <Title> <Last Name> should be considered.

More and more lists are being created with separate fields for a salutation and the recipient's first name. For example, many people named Robert prefer to be called either Bob or Rob. If the direct mailer gets the salutation right, the chance of a favorable response increases. Likewise, when marketing to older audiences, consider using the more formal <Title> <Last Name>.

The next level of personalization can involve the creation of specific messages and images designed to appeal to recipients from different geographic locations, ethnic groups, affinities (i.e., schools, sports teams, recreational activities, etc.), or just about anything else. Based upon the recipient's address, different dealers may be referenced in a communication and trade areas defined. The recipient can be directed to specific locations—i.e. retail outlets, local financial advisors, food and beverage locations, municipal charities, etc.

A subsequent step of personalization would relate to the recipients' last transactions or communications. In the not-for-profit realm, references to donors' last charitable dona-tions might be referenced with a suggestion for increased gift sizes. In the retail marketplace, last visits and/or pur-chases similarly could be referenced with additional buying suggestions. In the case of a retail purchase of a new camera, clever marketers could recommend batteries or film spe-cials. A financial services mailing might suggest a disability insurance purchase with the new college fund.

Laser Image Personalization

Here are descriptions of the four basic levels of laser image personalization:

Basic imaging. In its simplest form, laser imaging uses laser toner application technology to apply generic text and variable address information. In addition to the name and address block, a few words may also be variable depending on data fields containing geographic, socio-graphic, segmentation, or demographic criteria. Basic imaging personalization became prevalent during the early part of the 1990s.

Although many millions of pieces are still mailed with this level of laser imaging, it now fulfills only the lowest consumer expectation requirements. In order to provide the recipient with a more relevant message, direct marketers should con-sider stepping up their personalization effort.

Variable imaging. Variable imaging adds more personalization and customization capabilities than basic imaging. In addition to imaging basic information such as recipient's name, address, and salutation, variable imaging allows marketers to insert and subtract sentences and even paragraphs depending on whether or not database "triggers" are activated. For example, if a person's name was acquired from a list of outdoor magazine subscribers, a specific reference may be made to either the publication or an outdoor lifestyle. If the next recipient's name was purchased from a cooking magazine list, the customized information could easily change from an outdoor to a cooking reference. Variable imaging means that recipients receive information and images that are more likely to appeal to them based on captured database information.

Variable imaging of an address piece and personalized coupons in a pad form. (Courtesy DRAFT Canada)

Variable publishing. A true variably published document contains completely variable information from beginning to end. All images and text are specifically chosen for each recipient based on likely personal preferences. In addition to the content being completely variable, so is the layout. Consider a variably published newsletter. Not only are the text and images different throughout one production run, but also are the fonts, font sizes, number of columns, and even the masthead.

As long as the database has enough pertinent and accurate information to drive a variable publishing effort—this should be your first consideration—the final product can be an extremely meaningful piece of communication without resorting to low-value added personalization efforts such as slapping the recipient's name everywhere.

Full-colour variable publishing. A technology that has been developing for a number of years is full colour variable publishing. This technology can be toner- or ink-based, and allows the marketer to change every aspect of a printed piece, including colour. It is powerful because it can vary both text and colour images tailored to the recipient, but it is still a more costly endeavor. Due to its growing popularity, chapter 32 has been dedicated to colour laser imaging.

MICR Imaging

MICR (magnetic ink character recognition) is a form of laser imaging and a form of offset printing that is typically tied to the financial industry, most specifically with cheques. It consists of special characters made up of a special ink or toner. When a document that contains this ink needs to be read, it passes through a reader, which magnetizes the ink and then translates the magnetic information into characters.

⑈0⑈2045078⑈:⑈⑈02 ⑈⑈20⑈02045011⑈

As marketing intelligence increases, direct marketers will create a predictive model to offer services and products to close links upon past history and socio-demographic information. At this time variable imaging can cover all aspects of a mail piece from text to images.

Although variability and personalization are great marketing tools, they can also be a bit of a gimmick and come across as garish. All marketers should be cautioned about using too much personalization such as the recipient's name a dozen times but with no other pertinent information. A careful review of the accuracy of the database becomes paramount when more personalization is being considered.

PAL POINT... Personalization has come a long way. In the early days, it took an effort just to get the recipient's name at the beginning of a paragraph and have the rest of the paragraph wrap properly. With higher-level variable imaging and variable publishing, the old days are long gone.

Continuous Laser Imaging

Is your large-volume direct mail project appropriate for continuous laser-imaging equipment? Have you dodged this technology because of image quality concerns? Rest assured that today's exciting high-speed machines are appropriate for many of the finest long-run direct mail projects.

Continuous laser imaging is great for a wide range of high-volume direct mail projects including letters, order forms, statements, invoices, subscriptions, and self-mailers. Industries as diverse as financial services, the non-profit sector, business-to-business, and consumer products have had great success with this technology.

Reasonable Expectations

Are you concerned that continuous laser imaging machines don't have the resolution you need? Think again. Admittedly, some companies still use equipment with low-end resolution, but most have moved to 300 dpi, 600 dpi, or even higher. With the growing availability of high-speed machines, there is no reason to settle for less. Direct mail designers have a

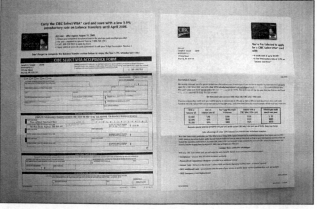

Sample of continuous letter/application. (Courtesy Euro RSCG 4D)

wide array of fonts to choose from because many companies are heavily invested in this vital area.

Higher printing resolutions mean your scanned logos, signatures, and halftones will look great. Because of incredibly low data storage costs, there aren't any significant limitations on the size of graphic images. In the rare case that a large image is unwieldy, your data processing professional can split and remarry it before generating output. Toner registration to offset printed forms is "dead-on" because continuous laser-imaging machines have accurate pin registration systems. (Occasionally, offset printing will move, but good laser imaging companies will attempt to "chase" the printing.)

Most equipment will accommodate two-up $8\frac{1}{2}\times11$-in. (216×279-mm)" letters. Since rolls of paper or fan-folded forms are used by continuous laser imaging machinery, the length of a form is theoretically infinite, although cutoffs typically range between 3 and 24 in. For large-volume jobs, you will save time and money if your laser-imaging partner has roll-to-roll equipment because it's faster and less costly than fan-folded or cut-sheet production.

Design/Layout Tips

When working with large solid areas of toner coverage, direct mail designers should ask for technical advice before committing to a design. Today's machinery can lay down rich 100% toner coverage for a while, but as the run length increases, consistent quality depends on how the solid areas are positioned on the form. In general, large solids running parallel (horizontal) to the perforations are OK, but those running perpendicular (vertical) aren't. Bad layouts may result in "toner starvation," which results in inconsistent and sometimes splotchy coverage. Be safe, and get advice from your data processing professional before signing off on risky and untested designs.

A common problem occurs when fan-folded stock is used and designers place copy too close to the perforations. Perforations form peaks and valleys as they pass over the drum, preventing toner from being properly applied. Combat this problem by positioning copy at least ½ in. (13 mm) away from all fan-folded (horizontal) perforations.

Paper and Ink

The paper you choose is important. Gloss coated stock is almost impossible to run on continuous laser-imaging equipment because toner cannot penetrate it, much less adhere. Fortunately, there are special stocks with glossy appearances that are porous enough to accept toner. Instead of naming specific enamel sheets, ask your mailing partner how the intended appearance can be achieved. Your mailing services company will try to help you get the look you want, decrease waste, increase productivity, meet deadlines, and lower mailing costs.

Tech Tip Once you've selected the right paper, make sure your offset printer uses heat-resistant, "laser-safe" inks. Forms that pass though high-speed continuous laser imaging equipment are exposed to high heat that will melt any and all wax present. Think of it this way: You wouldn't expect a candle to retain its shape in an oven. Don't expect the impossible from wax-based ink.

Diecut Forms

Direct mail jobs with die cuts can be eye-popping and beautiful, yet still run efficiently. However, there are a few caveats. Not only must diecut forms run well in high-speed imaging equipment, they also have to be compatible with other downstream machinery. Corners, edges, and other protruding points can cause problems on feeding units, saddle stitchers, inserters, commingling equipment, etc.

Kiss-cut jobs can be tricky. If the cuts are too deep, the carrier substrate may catch, resulting in frequent jam-ups. If the cuts are too shallow, the labels won't peel off as intended, rendering the product functionally useless. SMR•Tytrek once converted a 2,000,000-piece kiss-cut job. The diecutter had made the kiss-cuts too deep and SMR's high-speed continuous laser imaging machines jammed about every 1,000 cutoffs, or about 2,000 jam-ups in all. To make matters worse, some labels tore off and got caught in the drum cavity, which slowed production to a crawl and ruined several drums at about $1,000 each.

Tipped-on cards can be problematic too. If your direct mail job has a plastic or paper card tipped on, don't try to print too close to the edge of the card. Apply the $\frac{1}{2}$ in. (13 mm) rule here as well: Allow at least $\frac{1}{2}$ in. between the edge of the card and your intended copy. Less distance is possible, but your mailing services company should be consulted first.

Continuous Laser-Imaging Quality Assurance

Companies with high-speed continuous laser-imaging printers should have an extensive series of quality control procedures in place. According to an operations manager at a publicly traded direct mail services company, "Every hour, machines should be stopped, inspected, and cleaned if necessary. We continuously scan for problems such as voids, back grounding (excessive toner buildup on flash lamps), gray casting, cortron wire toner streaking, bad fusing, poor toner to ink registration, and wrong variable image content. In my department, we require every employee working on a job to do hourly sign-offs."

Maintenance is another important aspect of quality control. Regardless of whether continuous laser-imaging machines are maintained by an in-house staff or a third party, "24/7" coverage (24-hours per day, seven days per week) is essential. Today's direct mail deadlines are so tight that there is little if any scheduling slack. Continuous laser-imaging department heads know that if data processing falls behind on a job, every other department will have to scramble to make delivery dates.

Stock and Other Production Issues

If there's anything out of the ordinary with your paper, in general it's a good idea to run a test before beginning the main production run. For example, if you're running either a matte or textured stock through a continuous laser printer, test for proper paper feeding and toner adhesion. Likewise, if perforations are applied to the stock before laser imaging, make sure they're micro-perfs, or else test. Any glues present must be heat-resistant, or else the end user will end up with a sticky mess. And, just because you use wax-free ink, don't assume that it's laser friendly. Test all inks first, regardless of marketing claims.

PAL POINT... Laser imaging technology has made terrific advances. It wasn't too long ago that 240 dpi was the industry standard. Now, we're getting to the point where the difference between toner and offset ink isn't all that noticeable. This development has tremendous implications for the future of the direct mail industry.

Variable Colour Imaging—
Is It Finally Here?

Variable colour imaging (VCI) is the engine that drives one-to-one colour printing. The possibilities and applications of this exciting technology are endless.

VCI is a printed communication medium that can be specifically tailored to a recipient's demography, history (purchasing or otherwise), and anticipated wants/needs garnered from previous consumer behavior. Put yourself in the shoes of a boat manufacturer. Perhaps you want to send a mailing to a population of people that have indicated interest in a 32-ft. (10-m) cabin cruiser. Wouldn't it be great if you captured color and accessory preferences and sent everyone a printed mailer depicting their dream machine? How about helping an existing customer step up to a larger model? How effective would a promotional piece be if it showed a prospect's current boat next to an image of a larger, more attractive one? The local dealer could be identified with a map and a picture of a sales rep. This piece like this would certainly be compelling, and although it may not sell a boat by itself, it could be a vital keystone to developing a business relationship.

The concept of high-value-added personalization can be applied to many other products ranging from durable goods like boats, cars, and high-end appliances to intangible products like financial services. As our industry stands as of this writing, much of the outflow of digital variable colour is web-enabled. In some cases, it needn't be more than a fulfillment function where consumers log on to websites, key in buying interests and in a few days receive a mail piece tailored just for him or her. Corporate customers are developing web-enabled applications as the front end to facilitate front line parties with this power and influence.

Let's turn our attention to the automotive industry. Car companies maintain extensive records about their clients at both the corporate and dealership levels. Traditionally, mail pieces have been developed from the corporate level embracing the unique identities of each dealership but these promotions are frequently tied to a quarterly corporate time frame instead of the needs of each individual recipient. With the use of variable colour imaging and a web-enabled application, each dealership can now customize their mail pieces (within the guidelines of a predetermined template) to their specific clients and control the dissemination of the mail themselves to manage response flow during peak and slow periods.

These templates can pull from variable information such as a car's service history, last mileage reading and anticipated mileage (forecasting maintenance or other issues), dealership information such as hours of operation, deals on trade-ups or additional cars, preferred service numbers, and the service manager's name or the recipient's specific service advisor. All this information can be coupled with financial offers to create a truly effective one-to-one promotional piece.

This level of complexity requires the utmost in data integrity and proficiency during production. However, it would be foolhardy to ignore the people side of the equation. A project design team that thoroughly understands the flexibility and impactfulness of the variable world is essential. Project designers are no longer forced to place variable copy inside boxes, both figuratively and literally. The skill set necessary to accomplish wonderful things with variable copy is that of a good printer (for prepress, colour, and design) as well as a high-quality data processing facility in order to ensure accuracy. It is important that a vendor be chosen with the ability to link the two technologies.

Digital assets are supplied as they would be in an offset project and data should be supplied as it would in a data-driven program. But the two must marry up perfectly to be effective. Proofing and subsequent approvals require an eye for both. Attention to the printed detail and the variability of the sheet are both very important to the overall success of a project.

Admittedly, the issue of gathering all the images of products might take time. This is particularly true of many custom products with lots of parts. In the interim, as long as each communication contains basic service information, regardless of product, personalization will help customers realize that at least one company has taken the time to learn about them and their needs. While not the best solution, stock photography coupled with detailed customer information could still be effective for about a fifth of what it would cost to use completely customized images.

Yes, it is possible to create beautiful, completely customized VCI pieces for each and every customer and qualified prospect. However, practicality means that some compromises might have to be made. Rest assured that in time it will be commonplace to send mass mailings with as much personalized detail as the example detailed above.

Currently all but a few colours translate well in the VCI world since it is largely made up of process. Pantone colors are available but usually at additional cost. In general, try to start with four-colour process. Variable colour imaging can make sense on short runs such as daily fulfillment programs and large runs of a million pieces or more.

The three main pieces of equipment in the VCI market today are the Nexpress (Kodak), the iGen series (Xerox), and the Indigo (HP). The specifications of each are close, with sheet sizes ranging from 13.8×18.5 in. (350×470 mm) to 14.33×20.5 in. (364×521 mm) and 12.6×18.5 in.

TECH TIP As this book was in the final proofing stage, Indigo introduced a new web press, which has the potential to change long run VCI as we know it. Our point: As soon as the ink dries on this copy of *Direct Mail Pal—Canada*, there will be more changes. VCI is a new and rapidly changing frontier where the players are striving for the best possible products. Let's not kid ourselves: change will be fast and furious over the next few years.

(320×470 mm), respectively. As of this writing, the output is comparable across all three. The primary difference is that the Kodak and Xerox technologies are dry-toner-based whereas the Indigo uses liquid HP ElectroInk.

Back to the original question: Is variable colour imaging finally here? Not to unnecessarily complicate the question, both "yes" and "no" are appropriate. Yes, the technology has arrived; however, true VCI is too expensive for some projects. Don't think that variable digital colour is for every project. Use available data to achieve your goals. Do not just spit out variable colour because you can. In some cases, it may be more cost-effective to print shells and laser variable text and graphics in black-and-white. It is important to know when to step up to VCI.

PAL POINT... Fully robust yet cost-effective VCI still may be a few years away. Grow with the technology. Do periodic cost evaluations. These steps will allow you to have a better feel for the level of output available at any given time and help you make better VCI decisions.

33 Inserting Technology

For eighty years, high-volume mail inserting technology didn't change that much. Until recently, "swing-arm" style mail inserters dominated the Canadian lettershop industry and have done so since the early twentieth century. Although swing-arm machines still rule the roost in today's lettershop, a new design is emerging. These "continuous-flow" inserters are faster, more flexible in terms of single insert setups and are just as heavy duty as their predecessors.

Until recently, most high-volume heavy-duty inserting machine manufacturers stuck to their tried-and-true formula of gathering product and pushing it into envelopes. Although there have been some speed, reliability, and flexibility improvements made over the past half-century, they've been relatively minor. Swing-arm machines have had basically the same design for a very long time.

A Revolutionary Design

A recent design breakthrough is reinventing the mail inserting industry. These new continuous-flow machines significantly differ from swing-arm inserters. Consider pocket orientation. When swing-arm machines insert material into #10 envelopes, the inserts travel lengthwise during collation and insertion. On the other hand, continuous-flow machines gather product widthwise, enabling nearly twice as much material to be gathered at the same running speed. And, unlike office-grade equipment, the envelope opening device at the end of the production line is similar to that of the more rugged swing-arm inserter, allowing it to easily keep pace with pocket feeders during high-speed production.

These new continuous-flow machines are appropriate for high-volume manufacturing environments for three primary reasons. First, many critical parts are manufactured with industrial grade steel instead of lighter weight materials such as aluminum. Second, like other heavy-duty machines, they are easily adjusted and maintained. And third, the user-friendly, well-designed computer interface uses state-of-the-art electronics.

When they're running mailings with generic inserts, continuous-flow machines allow operators to set up "backup" pockets. Then, if the primary feeding pocket runs out of material or jams, the backup will immediately start to feed and will continue to do so until the primary one is reloaded or cleared. This backup pocket feature makes it much easier for operators to get production yields that actually approach maximum cycle speeds all day, everyday.

Continuous-flow machines have preprogrammed mainte-nance reminders scheduled right into the controller. Ignoring mundane tasks like lubrication and the changing of wearable parts is difficult to do, because messages flash on the com-puter screen at regular intervals describing precisely what actions need to be taken. Then, the controller automatically records what was done and sets a new alarm for the next scheduled maintenance item. Foolproof maintenance like this translates to less downtime and fewer missed customer delivery dates.

PAL POINT... According to a marketing study commissioned by PIA/GATF, direct mailers need to "improve the efficiency of the design and creative process, and increase its integration with the production requirements of direct mail." On the letter-shop floor, manufacturing flexibility and speed can help direct mailing professionals achieve their marketing objectives.

Automatic Label Application

One of the most frequently forgotten, but extremely versatile weapons in a direct mailer's arsenal are labels, commonly called Label-Aire, which is a brand of auto-mated label-affixing equipment, not the actual process. Label use is virtually endless, limited only by design creativity. The chances are good that the next time you open your mailbox you'll find a label on some promotional piece. If it catches your eye, you'll have technology developed by automatic label application to thank.

Common Applications

Every wonder how yes/no stickers, wafer-seals (tabs) closing gate-folded or short-panel folded products, brightly coloured labels cheering up black-only text and foil-stamped, and embossed or debossed labels are applied to direct mail packets? Yes, it's automatic label application.

Have you and your clients found yourselves in this bind: You need colour to sell, but your budget only allows for one-colour printing? A good compromise might be to apply a brightly coloured label on a one-colour laser-imaged product. You'd get the colour you need at a price you can afford.

Maybe your client has 25 stores and wants 25 different maps leading customers to each location. Since changing your plates on press 25 times is probably cost-prohibitive, perhaps apply-ing 25 different labels over a common direct mail piece will allow you to get the multiple lots you need at a price you can afford. Marketers love the versatility that labels offer because many special codes, unique offers and different attention grabbing devices can be tested at a remarkably low cost.

Automatic label application is wonderful for various situa-tions and can be a cost-effective method segmenting large production runs. We've seen clients take advantage of large volumes on equipment running "like" product. But for smaller subsets of the large run, labels were used to brand these subsets for different requirements. And because labels can be created on various colours and shapes, the end result was a cost-effective production run with a number of very unique segments that had their own specific identity via the use of different labels.

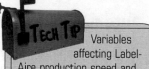

A Few Technical Tips

Even though today's automatic label application machinery can apply most labels within $1/16$ in. (2 mm) tolerance, nonetheless every job is different. It's best to involve your mailing services company early in the job planning stage. To prevent mistakes, discuss your job sooner than later and send an accurate representation of the piece prior to ordering labels. Good communication will prevent unwanted production surprises.

Rarely do large mail houses with lots of "redundant" machinery meet up against quantity restrictions. For example, at SMR•Tytrek in Toronto, many automatic label application jobs are run inline with other bindery operations at great speeds. Large companies routinely accept jobs running into the millions of pieces. Depending upon the actual equipment that is being used, labels can range from $1/2$ in. (13 mm) to $8^1/2 \times 11$ in. (216×279 mm), although the larger formats are fewer and farther between so it would be prudent to review cost and capacity with your chosen vendor.

PAL POINT... Whether you need to save a printing job (improper indicia, promotional date etc.), add a splash of colour to an economically printed piece or get multiple lots, you owe it to yourself to investigate the many benefits of automatic label application. Like so many other graphic arts processes, it's one of the little things that can put a competitive advantage in the pockets of those in the know.

35 Inside/Outside Inkjet Imaging on Saddle-Stitching Machinery

Where would the direct marketing industry be without high-speed, versatile inkjet imaging? Probably back in the days of paper labels and indiscriminate mass mailings. Improve the effectiveness of your next self-mailer, booklet, or catalog by using today's advanced inside/outside inkjet imaging technology.

Put some muscle behind your one-to-one direct marketing claims. Data mining techniques offer direct marketers vast pools of relevant information about the purchasing habits, preferences, and needs of virtually any target market audience. The first step is to find the right data. The second is to acquire knowledge of inside/outside inkjet imaging technology. The third is to design appropriate personalized communications and promotional materials that make good use of both data and technology.

What's Possible

Let's start with the basics. For years, direct marketers have known that different people respond to different messages. One-size-fits-all shotgun-style marketing methods don't achieve high enough returns to justify high production costs. Inside/outside inkjet imaging allows direct mailers to tailor their communications to address the needs, wants, and desires of their target audiences. Start by including the recipient's name, contact Information, and personalized message inside your self-mailing saddle stitched product.

Pre-filled-out order forms. Design your self-mailers, brochures, and saddle-stitched catalogs with pre-filled-out bounce-back vehicles such as tear-off business reply cards (BRCs) and order forms. Doing so will reduce the amount of response time needed. This is important because saving people as little as a few seconds can make a difference. Response rates will improve if fields such as name, address, account number, etc. are imaged on the BRC or order form. Response center clerks will have less data entry and will be able to process more orders. In addition, illegible handwriting problems should decrease, resulting in a higher percentage of responses that can actually be fulfilled.

Marketing codes. Marketing codes have a wide variety of sales and marketing uses. Customers responding to promotional materials by telephone frequently are asked for a marketing code printed somewhere on the piece. These codes enable easy tracking of marketing effectiveness. Also, prices and special offers can be code-driven and are easily changed as new marketing information becomes available.

Unique offers. Inside/outside inkjet imaging technology allows individual offers to be derived from information contained within individual recipient profiles. Different strings of text can be imaged based on factors such as previous purchasing habits, behaviors, credit history, and geography. For example, if a bank is soliciting new customers, as a purchase incentive, they may offer pocket calendars to people with historically low account balances, but pocket watches to their most attractive prospects.

Different telephone numbers and website addresses. Offering different service levels to different target audiences is appropriate for some businesses. A good example of this type of customer segmentation occurs in the airline industry. The major airlines have figured out how to enrich customer experiences based on an individual's frequency of travel, degree of loyalty, and profitability. Among other benefits, frequent fliers can use nearly wait-free telephone numbers and may

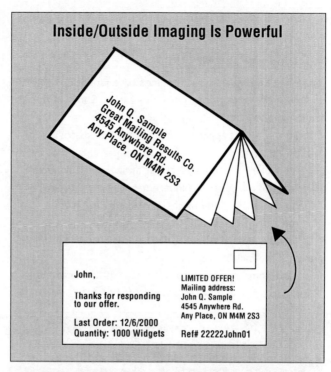

Inside/Outside Imaging Is Powerful

John Q. Sample
Great Mailing Results Co.
4545 Anywhere Rd.
Any Place, ON M4M 2S3

John,

Thanks for responding
to our offer.

Last Order: 12/6/2000
Quantity: 1000 Widgets

LIMITED OFFER!
Mailing address:
John Q. Sample
4545 Anywhere Rd.
Any Place, ON M4M 2S3

Ref# 22222John01

qualify for preferential check-in treatment. Think of your
business. If different phone numbers and website addresses
would make a difference, consider inkjetting a variable message
instead of printing a fixed message. This will reduce production costs and increase your marketing flexibility.

Lower postage. Properly designed inside/outside inkjetting
jobs achieve lower postal rates because of longer run lengths.
If you consolidate multiple shorter runs into longer ones,
your mailings will have more pieces per mailing, qualifying
you for better postal rate. For example, consider a 250,000
piece mailing in which your marketing messages are differen-
tiated by inkjetting. Instead of breaking up this job into smaller
offset printed batches, keep the entire run contiguous to

increase the percentage of your mail that attains the lowest cost Letter Carrier postage rate.

Some Technical Tips

Most inkjet imaging production lines have limitations regarding image size, placement, and run direction. Some of these are as follows:

- Inkjet ink is best applied to porous uncoated stock. With extra care and slower run speeds, it's possible to apply inkjet ink on coated paper, but at an increased cost. Solvent-based inkjet ink has inherent problems: toxicity and flammability being among them. Water-based inks are preferred because they're less costly and safer.
- On saddle stitchers, keep variable images on the inside at least three inches from the spine.
- Unusual fonts may need to be printed at low resolution. Ask your mailing services provider for advice.

PAL POINT... Lower your production costs and improve your marketing results with cutting-edge inside/outside inkjet imaging technology. Combine creativity, a healthy dose of pre-planning and multifunctional inkjet imaging to yield terrific direct marketing results.

36

Specialty Direct Mail Products and Finishing

Specialty finishing techniques enhance the physical aspects of direct mail projects. Regardless of whether your project looks like a diamond, has a pop-up, or folds in a special way, you've entered the exciting world of specialty direct mail finishing.

When planning a mail piece with specialty finishing, start with a physical representation of the intended product and back into design necessities. Ask your finishing partner, "What are the formats I'm restricted to on the mailer, folder, gluer, and saddle stitching-machine?"

Next, determine how the piece must be printed to suit the needs of the customer. If it is to be laser-imaged, what are the limitations presented because of this requirement? Find a physical form that is capable of meeting your promotional needs, yet can be efficiently and automatically produced. The more complex your project, the more you should work backwards from the conceived finished product toward the press and data work.

Finishing equipment and techniques abound in the direct mail industry. One of the biggest potential stumbling blocks is identifying a company that can turn your specialty idea into a physical product. Yes, some specialty machinery is probably necessary, but it's much more important to choose a finishing partner with an artist's eye and an engineer's precision in order to turn your concept into reality.

For example, gluing a shampoo sample onto a piece of paper is no huge feat, but gluing that shampoo sample onto a piece of paper with four-colour printing and variable imaging, while achieving maximum postal discounts via commingling and drop shipping programs, is truly special. Specialty finishing techniques can achieve eye-popping appeal, which may make all the difference when your piece is competing with a dozen other pieces in someone's mailbox.

There are very few cookie-cutter solutions. Instead, this chapter is intended to be a springboard for creativity. If you have a wild idea that you are trying to produce, ask a qualified specialty direct mail production expert for advice. Smart mailing services companies formulate solutions based on available tools and services, even when others say that what you want to accomplish is impossible.

Specialty Products—Explore Your Creativity

Specialty products often take multiple direct mail procedures and combine them with one or more specialty finishing procedures in order to create special physical effects. These types of pieces require careful design and engineering so that they can be efficiently produced and look good at the same time.

Some examples of specialty direct mail products include:
- Saddle stitching with inside/outside inkjet imaging
- Inline selective saddle stitching with inside/outside inkjet imaging
- Laser-printed signatures combined with sample applications in a self-mailer format

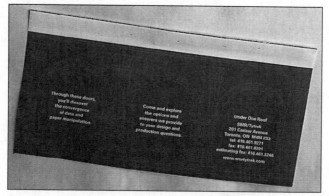

Sample integrated reply envelope. (Courtesy SMR•Tytrek)

A Partial List of Specialty Finishing Processes

- Cutting (in combination with another process)
- Folding (in combination with another process)
- Saddle stitching (in combination with another process)
- Trimming (in combination with another process)
- Folding and slitting
- Timed cutting—partial cuts and slits
- Timed perforating—partial perforations
- Glue application—permanent
- Glue application—release/fugitive
- Glue application—remoistenable
- Glue application—pattern
- Pocket creation
- Business reply envelopes (BREs)
- Zipper perforating
- Automatic label application (in combination with another process)
- Clip sealing
- Sample insertion (magnets, cards, CD-ROMs, and other data storage media, consumer product samples, money)
- Poly-bagging
- Shrink-wrapping

- Fully personalized sheets folded and stitched together with generic signatures to create a booklet that combine the cost-effectiveness of litho printing with the impact of personalized materials in a colourful package
- Duplex inkjet-imaged self-mailer with integral BRE and reply card
- Self-mailers with items affixed to them for impact or involvement
- CD packaging with uniquely coded inserts, shrink wrapped with an incentive label

If you intend on creating a piece that rises above the ordinary, start with a concept that has some flexibility in size, shape, orientation, etc. Reverse-engineer the piece starting with the final process and work backwards. Discuss your project's goals with your finishing partner and ask about their physical requirements. Once they have determined that the piece can be automatically produced, the previous step should be reviewed. At some point, postal regulations need to be assessed. You may find that extensive revisions are required to make the project practical. Finally, you should worry about whether the data will support the required personalization needed. Small conceptual errors can wreak havoc on the bottom line.

Tech Tip

Although an organization may have the basic bindery processes, if it does not have the experience and direct mail skills it may find itself out of its core expertise area. Look for organizations that can provide a history of creating unique products specifically for the direct mail industry and that have all the capabilities under one roof.

"Crack-open" self-mailer. (Courtesy Innovative Graphics)

PAL POINT... The specialty finishing design process can be streamlined by placing as many processes with as few vendors as possible. In addition, streamlining it also provides a level of confidence that the steps will dovetail correctly, thereby avoiding possible gaps in responsibility and accountability.

Cutting

37

Authors' Note: For the next four chapters, we're going to delve into the mechanics of four bindery operations: cutting, folding, gluing, and remoistenable gluing. Each is very important to the final appearance of a direct mail piece.

In direct mail, little things make a big difference. Success depends on good planning and paying attention to small details, like cutting. No matter which portion of the job receives the most attention, every process is vital to smooth production, meeting deadlines and making money. Think of a beautifully designed but poorly cut piece, perhaps one that has type running "uphill." Anyone who has experienced a problem like this knows what a disaster it can be. Cutting isn't a stepchild; rather, it's vital to success, or lack thereof.

Penny Wise, Pound Foolish

Some graphic arts production companies try to keep as much work in house as possible. Without getting into the pros and cons of outsourcing, do yourself a favor and keep the cutting, bindery, and mailing portions of your jobs together when possible. This will reduce unproductive finger pointing and increase vendor accountability. If a printer, for example, cut a job prior to outsourcing other mailing operations, they have by default accepted at least partial responsibility for the overall quality of the project. If their cutting is off, then so will be the folding, binding, and everything else that happens afterward.

Unlike three-knife trimming in which every side is uniformly cut, flat sheet trimming is difficult to keep precise. What appears to be good cutting during a production run may not be once the product is collated and the binding portion begins. At this point, small cutting variations between lifts may be very noticeable and likely will undermine the high-quality appearance you want. Regardless of whether you're comfortable with outsourcing, at least let those who do your mailing do your cutting too.

Paper and Ink Issues

In general, the harder the substrate, the more difficult it is to cut. Coated sheets with significant clay content have hard surfaces and require frequent knife changes, sometimes as often as twice a day. Recycled sheets can be difficult to cut because they contain a potpourri of paper fibers and miscellaneous waste. When cutting difficult stocks, it's hard to get clean, consistent cuts throughout whole production runs— no matter what precautions are taken. When problems occur, sometimes it's best to make sure your paper is the problem. Do this by substituting a different sheet. If the problem disappears, then it is indeed the paper. Then, take appropriate actions.

Some Technical Tips

Draw. The three main causes of "draw" problems are (1) wrong clamp pressure, (2) dull knife, (3) wavy stock, and (4) too thick of a lift of paper. Knives need relief as cuts are made or else sheets will be pulled. Full-sized lifts are fine for most porous stocks, but lift sizes should be reduced when cutting dense, heavily calendered paper with brittle clay

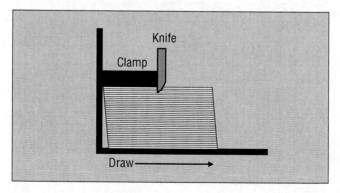

fillers. To maintain high-quality standards, lift thickness routinely needs to be reduced by 50%, or even more. Draw problems are especially noticeable on books with common images bleeding off pages, such as bars or lines. It's very important that printers work with bindery professionals that understand these trade-offs and are willing to make sure that all jobs are done right.

Tech Tip

If reflex blue or other slow drying colors are present on a sheet, brace yourself for more problems. Here is the Catch-22. If you use normal clamp pressure, you'll likely get excessive ink setoff. If you reduce clamp pressure to avoid this, knife draw problems will increase. The time to combat reflex blue ink is before the job even hits the bindery. Dry-trap-applied varnish usually works wonders.

Trim allowance. Even if your images don't bleed, try to avoid single chop cuts. The inherent problem with chop cuts is that you get one try and that's it. Once the cut has been made, there can be no more adjustments without reducing the final trim size. Cutting problems are magnified and affect folding accuracy and crossover image alignment. Whenever possible, allow at least 1/8" takeout trim margin.

True printers' guide and gripper. As diecutting and foil stamping experts know, easy identification of a press sheet's true guide and gripper saves time and reduces errors. The same holds true for cutting. If a sheet is converted in the same direction as it's printed, registration accuracy is much better. Sometimes guide and gripper sides are obvious, but at other times, they're nearly impossible to identify.

Gatefolds. Before beginning a gate-folded direct mail piece, cut a makeready lift, fold it and make sure the gap in the center is the right size. If the gap is too tight, you can still make adjustments. If it is too large and there are folds on colour breaks, you're stuck. If your cutting services company skips this makeready step, it is like they are cutting while wearing blinders.

Rotary scoring. When your job needs rotary scoring, score first then cut. Like die scoring, rotary scoring is more accurate when the true guide and gripper are still on the sheet.

PAL POINT... In recent years, the shortage of highly qualified cutting operators has fueled cutting technology workflow process improvements. Mail shop binderies need to maximize operator productivity to remain competitive. Large companies should consider dual cutting systems for high-volume direct mail work. On some jobs you can eliminate as many as five production people while simultaneously increasing output.

Folding

Accurate folding makes a world of difference in the direct mail industry. Look in your mailbox on any given day. Many printing projects with superb ink on paper don't look good because of poor folding. Nothing looks worse than sloppiness such as folds off colour breaks, bend-overs, or wrinkled panels. Coordinate your project with your mailing expert early in the planning stage. Potential folding problems can be prevented...if they are caught early.

Bindery work impacts a direct mail piece's appearance and performance as much as press, prepress, or lettershop work, yet it often is treated as an afterthought.

Plan for Success

Usually there are several ways to run any job. Simple layout changes can produce remarkable time and dollar savings. Panel size alterations and other minor design adjustments can make products look great, function better, and be more compatible with available production machinery.

Many folding jobs should have small variations in panel sizes, but don't. While the shape of individual panels may look similar, often they need to be sized differently to allow for shingling, wrap-around, washout (creep), and push-out. Paper is three-dimensional so don't ignore its thickness. Correctly designed panels will allow your bindery to fold the product on the colour breaks rather than along side of them. What looks

TECH TIP
For roll folds, the outer two panels should be final finished size with each succeeding interior panel decreasing by $\frac{3}{32}$ in. (2.4 mm). The last panel should be $\frac{1}{16}$ in. (1.6 mm) smaller than the preceding one. Failure to perform these steps can lead to bend-overs, bad color breaks, jams, waste, and increased spoilage.

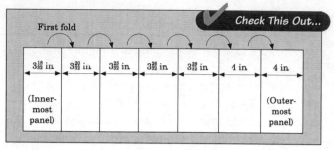

like sloppy bindery work really may just be poor design. Physical laws apply to folding. For example, don't expect your direct mail services company to produce an attractive multi-panel barrel-folded piece when equal-sized panels are stripped.

Always provide bluelines, rule-up sheets, bulking dummies, and a marked and sequenced folding sample (first fold A to A; second fold B to B; etc.). Leave ⅛ in. (3 mm) between copy and intended trim position and another ⅛ in. for takeoff trim. This allows for natural variation in both the printing and binding processes without risking product damage. Smaller margins are possible, but check first. Allow for washout when folding right angle pieces or when one sheet of paper is slit to nest. Your paper thickness will determine how much washout peeks out. Contrasting colors will make washout more noticeable, but careful preplanning can enhance a product's appearance.

Take Stock of Your Paper

In any product, there is some variation during the manufacturing process. Paper is no exception. Irregularities do occur and will affect folding performance. Inconsistent surfaces will contribute to decreased bindery performance. Even if a paper lot is uniform, there still may be great variation in paper bulk. For example, 80-lb. uncoated cover stock can caliper anywhere from 8 to 13 pt., depending on the manufacturer. This is significant because 10-pt. stock usually folds well while paper 12 pt. or thicker requires different folding techniques and machines. Be careful of running odd lots. Changing paper in the middle of a job will affect downstream folding so be sure to mark the change spot and advise your postpress partner.

An assortment of folded products.

Generally, the thicker your stock, the more variables you will face. Pre-score your stock if it is 110-lb. text weight or heavier. Sometimes thicker stocks without critical colour breaks can be in-line wet scored or folder scored, but always ask for an opinion before bypassing diecut scoring. When folding stock thicker than 10 points, watch for ripple cracking on buckle folders. A knife folder generally will not ripple-crack unless the stock is extremely thick, causing the sheet to fracture as it bends around the rollers.

Also, know your grain direction. Reduce cracking and the need for pre-scoring or inline wet scoring by folding your first fold with the grain. If this isn't possible, consider choosing a stock with short fibers and "off machine" coating for better moisture control.

Paper fibers can break during folding and result in cracking. Often, choosing proper fold-plates, machines, and production techniques can save jobs. The shock load on paper fibers

General Guidelines for Scoring

Offline channel scoring is recommended if your:

- Stock is 110-lb. text, 65-lb. cover, or heavier.
- Job's height/width or width/height ratio is greater than 3:1. (When thin rectangular sheets travel down a folding machine's side guide, they become unstable as they're jogged to the thin side. This is true regardless of the number of scores on a piece.)

Examples of width/height and height/width ratios

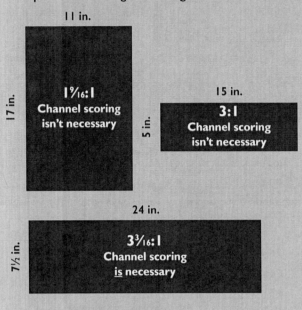

11 in.

17 in.

1⁹⁄₁₆:1
Channel scoring
isn't necessary

15 in.

5 in.

3:1
Channel scoring
isn't necessary

24 in.

7½ in.

3³⁄₁₆:1
Channel scoring
is necessary

Channel scoring isn't necessary if your:

- Job is printed on 90-lb. text or lighter, folds with the grain and has a height/width and width/height ratio of 3:1 or less.

Get scoring advice if your stock is:

- 100-lb. text or 60-lb. cover.
- 90-lb. text and folds against the grain.

increases geometrically with machine speed. So, when fibers are breaking, slowing down your folder greatly reduces fiber stress and many times eliminates the problem.

Ink Can Sink Your Job

If ink is too brittle, it may crack. Correcting this problem is difficult because ink has neither the strength nor flexibility of paper. Choose your fold plates and folding machines to minimize paper stress, add moisture to the surface (wet score), and slow down your folder. Wet ink is another common problem. If there is a good chance of having wet ink at bindery conversion time, use varnish or aqueous coating. Protecting jobs with reflex blue, metallics, or heavy black ink coverage resting against white paper after folding usually reduces smudging, scratching, and marking.

Varnish: Hero or Villain?

First, the good news: varnish seals ink and prevents marking and smudging.

Now, the bad news: A varnished sheet's surface is slippery and fold rollers have difficulty getting a good grip. Varnish dries to an uneven surface of peaks and valleys. When sheets run through folder rollers, the peaks are knocked off and ground into powder that gets on the rollers and alters their gripping ability. The exact point at which the rollers get a solid grip on the buckling sheet determines the position of a fold. If there is any change in the gripping characteristics of the rollers, the fold moves.

When a folding operator begins running a job, the rollers are clean and the job runs well. However, after a few thousand pieces, varnish powder is deposited on the rollers and begins to change the fold position. A knowledgeable operator will stop, clean the rollers, and watch the fold return to its proper position for another few thousand sheets. Or, a different operator may stop, change the fold stop position in the plate, and watch the piece quickly go out of folding register again. Either way, productivity and quality are very difficult on long run jobs with full (flood) varnish. For example, a non-varnished job that runs at 10,000 pieces per hour might yield only 6,000 or 7,000 if varnished.

Folding Potpourri

- Both wide- and small-gap gatefolds are possible. If you need a gap smaller than 1/16 in. (1.6 mm), or larger than a few inches, ask.
- "Green" projects can cause production problems. Soy ink tends to scuff more than regular petroleum-based ink. Recycled paper has a tendency to have less strength than pre-consumer paper because of shorter paper fibers, and it affects bindery performance. Recycled paper tends to be less pliable and is subject to more jams, increased tearing, a poorer quality fold, and more wrinkles.
- When using slitters, always check for clean edges. Asking your bindery about edge sharpness on multiple-up or folder trimming jobs is appropriate. For good product

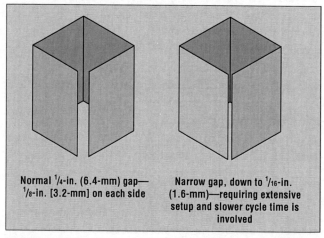

Normal 1/4-in. (6.4-mm) gap— 1/8-in. [3.2-mm] on each side

Narrow gap, down to 1/16-in. (1.6-mm)—requiring extensive setup and slower cycle time is involved

Double gatefold, with a normal gap (left) and a narrow gap (right).

appearance, do not use rotary knives to trim final folded enamel stock thicker than 0.024 in. (0.61 mm), or offset thicker than 0.028 in. (0.71 mm).

- For presses with dryers, consistent drying time is important because either oven temperature or web speed variation will lead to paper pliability and brittleness fluctuation.
- Allow your folding services company also to cut your job. You will substantially decrease transit problems and increase your yield.
- Properly band your skids to avoid shipping problems. If the stretch wrap is too tight, product corners can be damaged. For coated stock, band at right angles.

PAL POINT... Differentiate your direct mail projects with good folding. Be sold on the fold. Your customers are.

CHAPTER 39

Gluing

Many direct mail projects involve the application of glue, even if it is trimmed off during final conversion. Gluing is another behind-the-scenes bindery process that truly impacts direct mail production. Successful gluing requires a scientific approach and an artistic touch. The four horsemen of gluing—paper, ink, coatings, and glue—are about equal contributors to a job's success. Their combinations are nearly infinite and unexpected results do frequently occur. Sometimes easy-release (e-z) release glue tears paper fiber. Sometimes permanent glues perform like e-z release. Even the wizard Merlin would be puzzled.

Graphic arts glues are mainly oil, resin, or latex based. Each type of glue performs as expected most of the time, but there are more exceptions than anyone would like. Since glue is so important in many direct mail applications, we're going to explore production issues that can hinder project success.

Both e-z release and permanent oil-based glues offer good adhesive properties and are appropriate for physically heavy or varnished pieces. However, their relative great bulk may result in unattractive product from a marketing viewpoint. Resin-based permanent glues are cold applied and provide a good bond with a relatively small amount of residue. Latex e-z release glues are thin, generally reliable, inexpensive to apply, energy efficient (applied cold), environmentally friendly, and FDA approved for many food packaging applications. However latex is a natural rubber tree product and coagulates when contacted by steel, iron, or plastic. Coagulation can cause machine applicator problems. Also, latex glue doesn't work well in compressed air applicator systems.

E-Z Release Glue (a.k.a. Removable or Fugitive)

E-z release glue performs well 19 out of 20 times. But one tough job will prove there's no easy release from gluing headaches.

Common Uses for E-Z Release Glue

- Easy-release glue is an economical and attractive substitute for wafer sealing. (Properly manufactured products work great in the mail.)

- It keeps foldouts and gatefolds from unravelling during binding operations.

- It holds products together so that they can be automatically inserted (i.e., consumer product instruction sheets into bottles or boxes).

- It is great for pharmaceutical and/or miniature folded products.

E-z release glue performs best on penetration-resistant, highly calendered, dense paper with heavily inked and coated surfaces. Matte and other lightly calendered enamel stock, offset paper or sheets with a heavy clay fill are susceptible to delamination and fiber tearing when the intention is an e-z release effect.

Latex e-z release glues require long set up times (three to four minutes) and tend to spread when the opposing sheet is tightly squeezed. Their curing period is really 24 hours even though they appear to be dry after 10 minutes. Unfortunately, products that perform properly 10 minutes after manufacturing can change in 24 hours and pull fiber. Oil-based e-z release glues have a shorter curing time, but glue bulk remains an issue.

Managing variable adhesion and chemical reactions is important. Some e-z release glue solvents, such as ammonia, dissolve aqueous and other coatings and result in unintentional permanent adhesion. Occasionally, permanent resin glues can function as e-z release on aqueous coatings

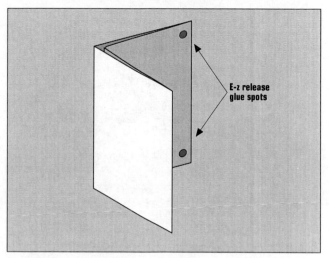

An example of e-z glue being used with a three-gatefold (also known as a "double gate") product.

because when dry they become very brittle and perform better than latex or oil-based e-z release glue.

Permanent Glue

Permanent gluing problems do occur, but are infrequent. For best results, select a paper with a porous surface and position the glue away from ink and coatings. Permanent glue needs to bite into paper, so the harder the surface, the more difficult it is to penetrate the sheet and create good adhesion. Knock out ink, varnish, UV, and aqueous coatings wherever you

Tech Tip

Often jobs require custom-made glues for special situations. You may need glue to penetrate a tough aqueous coating, work in high humidity, hold in freezing and thawing situations, or bind folded plastic while in a washing machine. A responsive supplier can save you hours of fruitless experimentation and help you meet deadlines.

An assortment of products that have been glued.

place permanent glue because glue tends to rest on top of coatings and cannot penetrate and grip fiber. Permanent resin glue spreads on stocks and coatings with a high barrier to penetration and can result in a poor bond or sloppy glue coverage. Absorbent and porous paper will allow glue to penetrate paper fibers and produce a strong bond. If gluing must occur over ink coverage, use wax-free ink. When stuck with a difficult permanent gluing job with aqueous coating, as a last resort, try using ammonia-based latex e-z release glue instead of permanent. It might just work.

Since water-based resin glues spread, those with critical glue registration require constant monitoring and sample pulls during production. Take special care when applying resin glue in a trim-out area. If glue reaches the paper's edge, sheets will stick together. Conversely, if glue spreads too far into the piece, it will not be removed during the final trimming process. If trim-out area is shorter than a ⅜ in. (10 mm), consider using e-z release instead of permanent glue because negative consequences of excess glue spread are less.

Machinery/Supplier Issues

Prior to the 1970s, gluing wasn't widely viable. Electronic systems that sense the presence of a sheet, wait a specified period of time, and then apply glue have made gluing practical. Most systems on the market now have pretty good electronics, but the next big advance in gluing technology is almost here.

Today's air-activated noncontact permanent gluing systems are extremely accurate and remarkably trouble-free. The capability to apply permanent glue from the bottom of a sheet is useful.

If your mail services company does gluing, make sure they're in frequent contact with their glue suppliers. Since most glue has a short shelf life, purchase and use glue biweekly to ensure good adhesive properties.

PAL POINT... Increase your likelihood of success. If you aren't gluing on a daily basis, get expert advice before beginning critical jobs.

Remoistenable Gluing

Until the 1990s, sheetfed printers had little opportunity to sell products with remoistenable glue. Today, short-run direct mail jobs with remoistenable glue are practical because the current crop of machines yield great quality and good production. Both sheetfed and non-heatset web printers now can produce products with direct response reply devices and participate in profitable direct mail campaigns.

There are primarily two ways of applying remoistenable glue. Cold application of water-soluble remoistenable glue—works by transferring glue to paper by either a wheel or a blanket. This process has two main advantages. First, heat by itself doesn't activate it, which means it is downstream laser-compatible. Second, glue application "pads" can be different sizes and run in different directions, which allows the efficient manufacturing of products such as three-sided "U" bar reply devices and stamps.

Unfortunately, there are some drawbacks with cold-applied glue. First, it has to be run through hot dryers, which frequently cause excessive paper curling and cracking. Second, cold adhesives tend to be thicker right at the beginning of the glue strip. Sometimes this thick buildup takes longer to dry and forces operators to choose between having either brittle paper or semi-wet remoistenable glue that may stick to neighboring sheets.

Extruded Glue

Hot-melt extrusion is the other way to apply remoistenable glue. These types of machines give operators more control over the placement and appearance of glue strips as they're being applied to the paper. Computer-controlled solenoids allow operators to precisely start and stop glue flow wherever necessary. For example, if a two-up piece is being glued on an 8½-in. (216-mm) side, an extrusion machine will detect

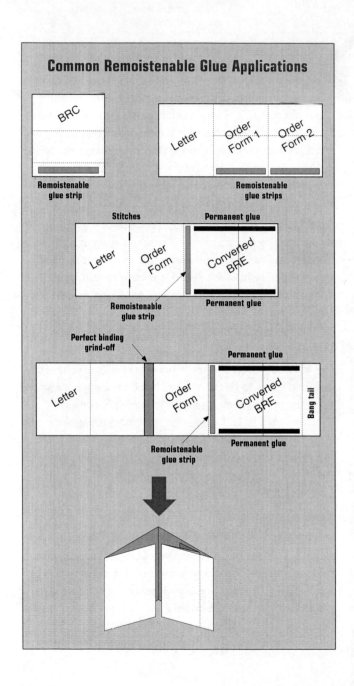

Common Remoistenable Glue Applications

BRC

Remoistenable glue strip

Letter | Order Form 1 | Order Form 2

Remoistenable glue strips

Stitches

Permanent glue

Letter | Order Form | Converted BRE

Remoistenable glue strip

Permanent glue

Perfect binding grind-off

Permanent glue

Letter | Order Form | Converted BRE | Bang tail

Remoistenable glue strip

Permanent glue

the presence of paper and begin the glue flow $\frac{1}{2}$ in. (13 mm) away from the paper edge. Then, it will apply glue for 8 in. (203 mm), stop for $\frac{1}{2}$ in., apply glue for another 8 in. and finally stop the flow $\frac{1}{2}$ in. away from the trailing edge.

Water-soluble glue applied on a pattern gluer can do this too, but since pattern gluers rely on timed entry rather than motion sensors, its application isn't as precise. In addition, extrusion hot-melt glues rarely curl paper and generally have a professional appearance while cold-applied glue looks duller, may have raggedy edges, and tends to curl since moisture is being added to only one side of the sheet.

A potential drawback of extrusion machines is that they can only apply remoistenable glue in parallel lines. This means that glue laid down in the shape of a "U" either needs two passes or two machines running inline at right angles to each other.

Inline Application

Many remoistenable glue jobs are done inline with other binding processes. For example, they may apply remoistenable glue, stop-perforate the sheet, apply seam glue to form a pocket, fold it (barrel folds, accordions, and gatefolds), apply wafer seals, slit it, and keep the job in mail-sort order—all inline. Needless to say, inline production greatly reduces turnaround times and cost, making non-heatset web and sheetfed companies competitive on many jobs.

TECH TIP If you have a form with side-by-side envelopes, don't have the glue strips rest against each other as they're coming off machines. Unintentional adhesion can occur when glue strips are directly in contact with each other face to face, especially during shipping. Staggering designs so that glue strips avoid contact with each other is a much better way to plan a job.

Regardless if the piece is a self-mailer, or will be bound into another product, inline production is a good value.

Avoid flatbed trimming after remoistenable glue application because it may cause a series of three problems. First, productivity will decline because sheets will have to be cut in very small lifts in order to clamp properly and not tear due to inadequate clamp pressure. Second, glue bulk will raise a bump in each lift resulting in the top sheets being longer than the bottom ones after trimming. Third, cutting through remoistenable glue wreaks havoc on knives; especially those super-hardened for long life.

PAL POINT... Remoistenable glue makes many direct mail programs better. Printed pieces with easy ways to respond are more effective than those without. In summary, remoistenable glue makes response mechanisms easy and quick to use.

Tipping

A long standing goal of direct mail project planners is differentiation. One way of differentiating your piece from all the others in cluttered mailboxes is to encourage the recipient to "involve" themselves with your piece by removing or unsticking something temporarily "tipped" (attached) to the main piece (carrier substrate). Examples of tipping include sample packets (shampoo, gum, mints, etc.), magnets, CDs, stitched booklets, or formed boxes.

Involvement pieces certainly have eye appeal, however production complications can arise and must be preplanned carefully. Even with the guidelines listed below, the authors encourage you to make your production partner an integral part of the planning process.

Key Factors to Consider When Planning an Involvement Piece

Size. Both the piece being tipped on and the carrier substrate must be within the manufacturing constraints of the equipment being used. If you are using a pre-existing piece such as a mustard sachet sample, this will be the starting point and your carrier will need to be developed to accommodate the sachet. When engineering tipped on involvement pieces, packets such as this mustard sample are the predetermined components and thus are the starting point.

Adhesion. Glue adheres much better to stock free from press-applied coatings such as ink, varnish, or aqueous coating. For permanent or remoistenable gluing jobs, the first step is to make sure that the area of the paper to receive the glue has all ink and press-applied coatings "knocked out" for adhesion purposes. For a tipping project, the right adhesive must be chosen for proper adhesion until the piece being tipped on is removed by the end-user. The balancing act is that there must be enough adhesion to ensure the product is attached through the mailstream, but doesn't rip paper fiber upon removal. Various glues have many different adhesive properties and need to be carefully chosen for each tipping situation. Your production planning team needs complete information in order to make the right selection. User intent, glue selection and paper substrate coatings are the three key factors to get right.

Product packaging. When planning a job with a piece to be tipped on, all "downstream" machine operations must be carefully planned. As already discussed, tipped pieces come in a variety of sizes and shapes and need to be efficiently fed in machines without excessive snagging and stoppage of expensive production lines. Concise and uniform packaging of the materials is crucial to successful production. Most of the time, product should be ordered in single rows and layers, using cardboard separators as necessary. This may require special instructions to a manufacturer who wouldn't normally perform this operation, so explicit written instructions are mandatory. Visit the component manufacturer if you can and develop a good working rapport with a production representative to ensure both companies understand the other's needs.

Shipping. Carefully consider the shipping method and the time of year to factor the tolerances and conditions under which these may be shipped. Glues have both melting points and cracking points. When stored or transported in high heat, remoistenable glue can reactivate, creating undesirable "bricking" of product. In colder temperatures, e-z release glues may become brittle and lose their adhesive properties.

PAL POINT... Carefully review how the tipped component will be handled in all production manufacturing stages. Consider how it will be fed in various machines and choose your adhesives wisely. Ensure that all glues will not react in undesirable ways with any part of the job.

Integrated Cards and Labels

New markets are constantly turning to integrated cards for a more cost-efficient alternative to mailing plastic cards. The mailing of plastic cards was made popular by the credit card industry, which sent cards attached to accompanying correspondence. Obviously, the weight of the card or other attachable collateral items such as magnets adds to the cost of mailing in terms of both materials and production.

The use of integrated cards, however, has greatly reduced the cost of putting these cards in people's hands. Now entities ranging from nonprofits to health clubs use integrated cards for loyalty programs, membership ID, and more.

Using most printers, custom cards can now be printed directly onto documents. Here's how it works: Say your company insures automobile drivers. You start with a document, called the carrier. In this case, the carrier is a letter that welcomes newly insured customers. You print the carrier and apply a laminate to the backing, known as a back patch or under-laminate. A laminate can be added to the front (a face patch or over-laminate) as well. Next, you diecut a card shape through the over-laminate and carrier. The back patch allows the card to be easily peeled from the carrier. Now you mail the letter and the card as a single piece. The card is the recipient's new auto insurance policy card, and is sturdy enough to be stuffed into a wallet.

All of these procedures can be performed inline by a couple of manufacturers like Relizon, creating a meaningful and useful, customized direct mail piece. Typically integrated cards are credit card sized. However, they can be as small as a penny or as large as the application demands, within the limits of standard paper and mail sizes. Several cards can be placed on a single sheet, allowing for multiple targets at a single address, such as one card for each member of a family or for different kinds of offers that might be activated at different times.

Integrated Labels

The production of integrated labels is the same as that for integrated cards. Integrated labels offer strong adhesiveness to bond to most carrier stock, yet are easily removable from the attached form. Think of the cost-saving advantages. Integrating the label into the document

TECH TIP

Integrated cards are not affixed to the base documents, or carrier, the way credit cards are; therefore, they result in a thinner product that is imaging and processing friendly and stacks easily. Under- and over-laminates make integrated cards water and wear and tear resistant. Also, the card stock can be the same as the carrier for a uniformed appearance.

helps eliminate errors and the need for extra data entry. Labels can even be formatted to match the colour of the carrier document to extend branding.

Whether you are planning to use integrated cards or integrated labels, or both, there are a few variables to consider prior to beginning the process. Discuss with your direct mail provider the intended use and lifespan of the card and labels.

To be cost-effective, your direct mail house might suggest minimum runs of 20,000 pieces and up. Lead times will extend three to four weeks for production.

PAL POINT... Even if your business does not issue membership or identification cards, consider adding integrated cards and labels to your direct marketing strategy. Think about starting affinity and discount programs, using the integrated cards to entice customers to join up or renew their relationship with you. Also, integrated cards and labels can be printed with up to six colours and logos, keeping your brand in front of prospects and customers.

43

Matching and Converting High-Volume Mailings

Here's a question that doesn't need a rocket scientist to answer: If the goals of a marketing program can be accomplished at either low or high cost, which is better? (Hint: We're looking for a three-letter word here.) To be successful at keeping your costs low, do yourself a favor and involve a direct mail planning expert early in the conceptual stage, especially when working on new matched mailing projects.

Let's assume you're working on a routine 200,000-piece, four-page, 8½×11-in. (216×279-mm) solicitation letter with personalization on each of the pages (two sheets). Your layout can make a big difference in terms of production costs. There are three possible ways to approach this type of project:

1. **Sheetfed**—a single sheet of 11×17-in. (279×432-mm) paper is produced with pages 1 and 3 beside one another and 2 and 4 on the reverse. Once lasered, the single sheet is then slit to yield two 8½×11-in. pages, interstacked, and finally folded to the desired size (i.e., in half to fit a 6×9-in. [152×229-mm] envelope or in thirds to fit a standard #10 envelope).

2. **Sheetfed**— a single sheet of 11×17-in. paper is produced with pages 1 and 4 beside each other and 2 and 3 on the reverse. Once lasered, the single sheet is then folded to 8½×11 in., folded in half or thirds (depending upon envelope size) and a small gutter is slit off, removing the folded edge and yielding two sheets, four personalized pages matched and folded together.

3. **Continuous form**— a 11×17 in. (18 in. [457 mm] if you include pinfeeds) is produced with pages 1 and 3 beside one another and 2 and 4 on the reverse. Once lasered, the continuous form is then slit to yield two 8½×11-in.

pages, interstacked (and kept in registration by way of the pinfeeds), cut at the 11-in. cutoff, and finally folded to the desired size (i.e., in half to fit a 6×9-in. envelope or In thirds to fit a standard #10 envelope).

Each process has its merits, but ultimately no. 1 is the most complex and costly, and no. 3 is the fastest and most cost-effective process. There are those who may try to produce two separate, personalized sheets and try to marry them as they are being folded by way of optical character recognition (OCR), barcodes, or matching. Although these are options, the addition of OCR or barcodes will add costs and the commensurate marking may be perceived as unsightly by marketers (these technologies are often reserved for multi-page and variable-page bills and statements). The use of matching a project like this does bear some risk as far as mismatching is concerned.

Form Separation
Separating forms used to be a standalone and relatively costly process. However, machinery advances in folding and

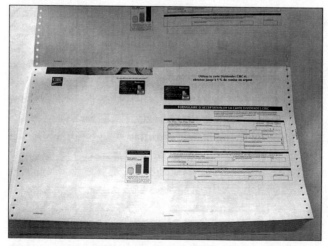

Sample continuous form. (Courtesy Euro RSCG 4D)

other inline processes have significantly contributed to making form separation faster, less costly and more efficient. Regardless of whether your forms are imprinted roll-to-roll or fan-folded, they need to be separated. In most cases, fan-folded forms and roll-to-roll forms are cut apart on document converters. Previously, forms were often "burst" apart at the perforation between forms. A burst form looks very much like a direct mail solicitation.

If you are trying to create letters and reply devices in standard sizes, such as an 11-in. (279-mm) letter and 3-in. (76-mm) reply device on the same stock that could be printed on the same form, the best way to run this job would be to place both it on an $8\frac{1}{2} \times 14$-in. sheet, gatefold and slit the piece (slit-to-nest), which completely eliminates the matching of separately printed components. Although this is the simplest format, there are others that can be designed with the help of your lettershop to create letters, replies, and buckslips, all matched and mechanically imaged and folded together. Yes, "intelligent" inserters with barcode readers can accomplish this same result, but why spend the additional money? In general, high-volume matched mailings are most efficient when personalized components are printed on common forms and converted inline while keeping proper sort order.

Cutting Edge Technology

For mailing jobs with multiple matched components, intelligent inserters or sophisticated inline conversion machines deserve consideration. As an example of how powerful the later can be, it's now possible to simultaneously image, trim, fold, tuck, glue, marry, and insert up to seven personalized components. While there are different ways of accomplishing this feat, it's only practical for very large and frequently repeating matched mailing jobs.

There is another class of equipment specifically designed to handle statements with randomly varying page counts. These "statement converters" are appropriate for credit card statements, phone bills, or other similar types of mailings. With the help of end-page record locaters, sophisticated scanning technology and holding "reservoirs," statement converters can easily handle a one-page credit card bill followed by a seven-pager and then a three-pager. These machines are investment-intensive and usually involve cut-sheets, not continuous forms.

PAL POINT... Savvy marketers are always on the lookout for ways to tweak their project specifications to get the most bang for their direct mail buck. In many instances, personalization and message customization help increase response rates. However, if matched mailings are poorly designed, production costs can spin out of control. In today's competitive direct mail landscape, there isn't much wiggle room for layout mistakes— so get it right!

44

Poly-Bagging and Shrink-Wrapping

Nothing gets printed pieces through the mail more safely, attractively and inexpensively than poly-bagging and shrink-wrapping. Companion pieces can be bundled together, big or small, thin or thick, in virtually any order, while keeping proper mail order sequence.

Both technologies are gaining ground in Canada. In Europe and some parts of the United States, it is already everywhere. There, promotional materials, newsletters, magazines and many other printed materials have been poly-bagged and shrink-wrapped for years.

Here are some benefits shared by both poly-bagging and shrink-wrapping:

- **Clear packaging.** Clear poly-bags and shrink-wrap let the beauty of printed pieces show through packaging. Paper envelopes cost more and hide the package's contents. Sometimes this is a good thing, but often it isn't.
- **Protection.** Both poly-bag and shrink-wrap film comes in many thicknesses. Choose the one appropriate for the heft of your package being bound. Excessive moisture and banging around wreaks havoc on traditional packaging. Some companies have enclosed poly-bags into fertilizer bags. Try that with paper envelopes!
- **Environment.** 100% recyclable film is now widely available.
- **Thick bundles.** High-speed shrink-wrapping and poly-bagging technologies can accommodate bundles as thick 2 in. (51 mm) or more.

Poly-Bagging

The poly-bagging process isn't complicated. Technically speaking, you can think of the production process as "poly-wrapping," whereby a poly-bag is formed around stacked product and heat-sealed on the front. A continuous "tube" is created around the product, and is sealed and separated as the tube travels down a conveyor belt.

For all but the smallest runs, poly-bagging is inexpensive. If makereadies are spread over 100 pieces, poly-bagging costs a lot. So does everything else. At about 10,000 pieces, poly-bagging starts to make sense. Once you're doing 10,000 or more, other protection methods seem impractical. For example, inserting materials into large paper envelopes costs a lot more and in many people's opinion doesn't look as nice. Even the fastest automated shrink wrappers rarely exceed 2,000 pieces per hour while poly-bagging machines can routinely run at 7,000–10,000 per hour, depending upon insert number and size.

Common direct mail applications for poly-bagging include promotional materials, newspaper inserts with free samples, magazines packaged with accompanying pieces, computer publications with free software, piggy-backed periodicals, atlases with maps, subscription renewal notices, brochures, statements, and invoices.

Poly-bagging is versatile. Since a poly-bag is built over stacked product, you have much more flexibility when midstream job changes happen. For example, if a thick onsert needs to be added to a portion of a poly-bag project, pre-purchased envelopes may not be usable. However, with poly-bagging, your project should be fine. Also, since poly-bag shuttle feeders and loading pockets accommodate wide varieties of object shapes and sizes, many consumer products may automatically be fed. Similarly, conveyors can turn pieces at a right angle. Therefore, spine and folding edges no longer need to run parallel with the poly-bag seam.

Poly-Bagging Design and Production Tips
- Before printing your address panel, remember that indicia and address label positioning usually runs parallel to the spine edge of normal sized mailings—not adjacent.

- More and more poly-bagged packages now contain person-alized content. These projects must be carefully planned.
- While it's not mandatory, try to have your carrier (bottom) piece be the largest and sturdiest of the package.
- The poly-bag seam is usually between 1 in. and 2 in. (25 and 51 mm) wide. For aesthetic purposes, it can be positioned to suit your needs, but there are limitations especially when printed poly is involved.
- Chop seals on both ends of your poly-bag need an allowance of at least $\frac{1}{2}$ in. (13 mm) each for excess film. This requirement increases proportionately as the bundle gets thicker.
- Before applying paper labels directly to the poly-bag, insist that your poly-bagging services company test adhesive strength prior to production. Poly film is a petroleum-based product and can have complicated glue adhesion properties.
- For printed poly, keep metallic inks away from sealed edges.
- If your mailing project is unusual in anyway, play it safe by getting a pre-production sample approved by your local postmaster.

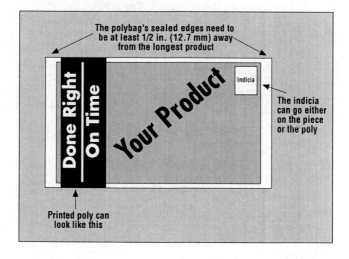

The polybag's sealed edges need to be at least 1/2 in. (12.7 mm) away from the longest product

Done Right On Time

Your Product

Indicia

The indicia can go either on the piece or the poly

Printed poly can look like this

Shrink-Wrapping

Shrink-wrapping is similar to poly-bagging in that it protects and holds multiple products together. However, shrink wrap film usually is thinner and less sturdy than poly-bag film. Shrink wrap's main attraction for some direct mail project planners is its lack of a seam running the length of the product. Also, the shrink-wrap process creates an extremely tight, glossy package. This provides an unrestricted view of the package contents. It has become the protection method of choice for high-end products. Think of poly as an overcoat and shrink wrap as a second skin.

Poly-bagged products.

Many shrink-wrapped products are successfully sent through the mail. However, usually the mailing information is either printed on the product itself or on a separate sheet laid on the top of the package. Keep in mind that if you are looking for the most brilliant result, then shrink wrap is probably the best solution. Shrink wrap typically has a greater sheen and clarity than poly wrap. The cost of shrink wrapping is comparable to that of poly-bagging.

PAL POINT... If you're still skeptical about the additional cost of either shrink-wrapping or poly-bagging, verify its power for yourself. Go to your local post office and watch people interact with their mail. Notice a lot of unopened envelopes getting tossed? Sure. What about poly-bagged or shrink-wrapped packages? They get opened...nearly every time.

Mail Security*

Direct mailing professionals know that their number one job is to get recipients to open the envelope sent to them. No longer is the colour of the envelope or design of the insert the only element of a mailing you must consider. Now, vigilance to safety and security throughout the business world has helped to shape a new paradigm for direct mailing professionals.

Communicating credibility is a top priority. Methods to ensure the safety and security of direct mail documents can be used at each stage of the process—from printing to production to the actual mailing. One of the most telling indicators of credibility is the method by which the mailing is posted. Metered mail, which is a core offering of Pitney Bowes, and permit mail, which is mail posted according to a special licensing arrangement with a postal authority, both allow the recipient to ascertain the identity of the sender with or without opening the letter or package.

Direct mailers need to take an active role in the management of their mail centers and those of their vendors. The mail center is the informational hub of every company, and individuals working in it have direct impact on both incoming and outgoing mail. In fact, mail center staff serves multiple roles—from gatekeepers to information resources. In order to ensure that these employees are capable of dealing with all aspects of mail security, each should be thoroughly screened. Mail center employees have access to sensitive information, including details about the financial and personnel status of other employees. By using legally approved screening

---

*Adapted from Pitney Bowes "Securing Your Mail System," reproduced with permission, Pitney Bowes, copyright 2002.

methods, such as drug screens, criminal background checks, and reference and employment history inquiries, you can be assured that the mail center staff is equipped to handle its responsibilities. Since many of their tasks require specialized knowledge, all mail center employees should be continuously trained, updating procedures and informing staff of new developments to ensure all mailings comply with CPC regulations.

Outsourcing is one way to manage the direct mailing process. Because of the commitment mail center management involves, some companies choose to outsource this function to professional firms who specialize in on-site training and technical support. These are mail experts with proven experience and expertise. Working with these consultants, you can improve accuracy and efficiency through trained staff and the latest mail production technologies. In addition to staffing and equipment, consultants can help perform an audit to ensure that your mail center is properly access-controlled and that only authorized personnel handle the mail. Going one-step further, direct mailing professionals can also choose to outsource all mail center functions. For example, Pitney Bowes manages more than 1300 mail centers worldwide. The company's outsourcing can be done on or off-site, depending upon your needs.

Other Things to Consider

In addition to the use of metered mail, a secure mail center and outsourcing experts, direct mailing professionals should always consider the reaction of the recipient when designing their mailings. Status-quo processes may need to be changed if they can in any way be perceived as a security breach. Here is the takeaway message:

> *All direct mailings must instantly communicate that
> the sender is credible and legitimate—from the
> inclusion of a company logo, return address, or
> alternative contact information (e.g., toll-free
> number, website address) to a cellophane window
> that allows recipients to view the contents of the
> envelope.*

All of these elements contribute to a new class of "intelligent mail" that is tailored to meet the needs of senders and recipients. The key is for direct mailing professionals to design and forward mail in a safe and secure manner that encourages the recipient to open the materials. With the partners, technology and resources available today, it is very easy for you to get the assistance you need to do so.

PAL POINT... Use a postcard or an inexpensive mailing piece to inform your customers and prospective customers about the steps that you have taken to secure your mail center and the mail they receive from you.

46

Sometimes Downstream Induction Is Necessary

What Is Downstream Induction?

Downstream induction typically relates to Unaddressed Admail. A mailer can save a portion of postage by fulfilling the transportation aspect of mail delivery themselves. The norm with Unaddressed Admail is to induct all mail into one central plant and CPC handles the task of transportation through the postal system and into the downstream postal stations.

By assuming the responsibility a mailer can save the transportation charges by delivering Unaddressed Admail to the downstream stations via their own trucks or privately contracted transportation company. Sometimes the impetus to do this is based upon cost and sometimes it is based upon timing.

For Addressed Admail there are no postal savings, leaving time as the only reason to induct Addressed Admail downstream. Due to the lack of postal savings it is very expensive. However, there have been situations where a communication must arrive at a certain time and the best manner to manage the flow of mail is to bypass CPC routing and induct it into the postal system at the downstream plants

Timely In-Home Deliveries

Less CPC handling means mail gets to its destination faster and more predictably. Bypassing the local Post Office means that there is a lot less chance for mail to be delayed. On average, downstream induction can save between one and four days on the in-home delivery.

Downstream induction is not for everyone. Some companies insist that their mail must enter the CPC postal stream on a particular day, regardless of impact on in-home delivery dates. Those who need the security of a postal receipt showing that mail was delivered to a postal facility on a particular day shouldn't even consider downstream induction. However, if fast delivery and effective in-home dates are a requirement, look into the option of downstream induction.

Materials Handling and Logistics

The best direct mail professionals are on a never-ending quest for the fastest, cheapest, and sexiest solutions.

Companies that convert product from one form to another need good materials handling and warehouse management processes. In addition to performing data processing and production services, direct mailers take physical job components and add value by cutting, folding, addressing, stitching, and otherwise changing the shape and form of mailing components. However, getting good machine production is only part of the operational equation. If machines are operating at peak efficiency (fast production, low spoilage, good quality, etc.), but are held up because of poor material flow, the end result is bad productivity rates.

Due to the complexity of many direct mail projects, attention to detail is very important. Small companies that employ a few people may be able to get along without formal inventory tracking. Past this size, these systems often are essential. Without state-of-the-art material handling systems, large companies can and often do waste countless hours looking for missing components, pallets, etc.

Materials Handling Tips

- **Strapping and wrapping.** All pallets should be properly strapped and wrapped. Coated stock with a slippery surface can, and sometimes does, slide off pallets. When this happens, re-stacking the job is a costly and time-consuming affair. Don't cut corners: Strap and wrap all pallets well.

- **Double stacking.** Pallets with paper should not be double stacked. No matter how careful forklift drivers are, damage will occur. Compensating for bent or crushed corners increases the amount of time required to load machines and reduces productivity.

- **Skid tags.** Use placards on every pallet to properly identify its contents. While skid tags are always important, they are especially so when two or more job components are placed on one pallet. Reducing freight costs by "mixing" pallets makes sense, but if they're not clearly marked, the savings can easily be lost. To prevent pocket loading and other yield-reducing problems, machine operators must be able to quickly identify a job's components. If you use mixed pallets, identify component breaks by placing separators between the material—especially when the components look the same.

- **Carton packing.** Choose the right carton size and gauge and pack all boxes tightly. "Transit" marking—spots where ink is scuffed or partly rubbed off—is the result of excessive product movement during shipping. For example, if a 12-in.-tall (305-mm) box is filled 11 in. (279 mm) high, product will jostle and rub as trucks turn and go over bumps. Even if poorly packed jobs escape transit marking problems, they still may end up with bent corners causing machine jam-ups, reduced yields, and increased manufacturing costs.

- **Ink issues.** Be careful of direct mail components with heavy ink coverage on one side of the sheet and light coverage on the other. Anytime a lot of ink rests against white paper, the chances of undesirable marking increases, either during shipment or pocket feeding. The problem is even worse when reflex blue is used because it dries so slowly. Other inks causing concern include some reds, purples, and metallics.

- **Print less.** If direct mail project managers and their business partners pay careful attention to material handling issues, spoilage will be reduced. After a few months of consistent and documented spoilage reduction, it may be possible to reduce print quantities by a percentage point or two.

Advanced Racking Technology

Racking is a type of materials handling and warehousing system with many benefits. Although companies pay for the cubed volume of their buildings, frequently they don't use all their available floor-to-ceiling space. Advanced racking technology allows forward-thinking companies to house materials all the way up to the ceiling without stacking pallets or damaging product. Going up, instead of out, reduces forklift travel distance, saving time and labor hours. Racks bolted into cement floors also serve to protect pallets from errant forklift damage.

A 50,000-sq.ft. (4,600-m^2) warehouse once could accommodate only 3,000 pallets. However, a $300,000 investment in a state-of-the-art racking system will increase capacity to 7,500 pallets in the same space. Although this investment sounds expensive, it is a whole lot less than putting up a 75,000-sq.ft. (6,900-m^2) addition to the warehouse.

Racking systems with special "narrow aisle" forklifts reduce aisle space needs, allowing more racks to fit in less space. Some only require 10-ft. (3.05-m) aisles between double rows of racks, instead of the customary 12 ft. (3.66 m).

If any of your vendors are thinking of installing a new racking system, encourage them to buy one that uses a standard 40×48-in. (1016×1219-mm) pallet size. Doing so means you won't have to worry about coordinating any production changes between your vendors.

PAL POINT... Many businesses treat their warehouse like an unwanted stepchild. Although materials handling is ripe with potential costs savings, frequently it's last on the resource priority list. This is a mistake, because good product flow is vital for efficient manufacturing. In short, effective materials handling processes lower direct mail costs.

Track A Mailing

48

Direct mailing professionals need timely deliveries and good information. To help, CPC has developed system called Track A Mailing that allows mailers to track how their projects are doing as mail processing occurs. This technology is in the process of being implemented, currently at level 1, and by the time of this book being in print it is hoped to be widely available.

In the near future, Addressed Admail Letter Carrier Presort (LCP) mailings will be able to be tracked from order creation to container destination processing points. CPC tracking systems will be able to label each mail container uniquely, place it in the system and then keep a tracking record of where it has been, how long it was there, and when it actually arrives at the final destination. This system will improve service levels by offering detailed management of mail trays as they track through CPC. Over time the system will be able to identify problem areas; thus enabling CPC to make improvements while offering direct mail providers important information about existing trouble spots.

PAL POINT... Since July 2004, CPC customers have been able to access tracking information of oversized priority packages using the On-line Business Centre on Canada Post's website under "Track a Mailing." Addressed Admail (LCP) customers who want to benefit from this new technology will have to use the CPC Electronic Shipping Tool (FST) to prepare and submit orders.

Response Management

Before your mailing has been sent, and certainly before any response has been received, it's critically important to have a carefully constructed response processing system in place. This is the mechanism that ensures that the prospect receives timely communication while the request is still relevant. Regardless of what type of fulfillment is required—more product information, telephone call, sales visit, etc.—timeliness of response is where some direct response programs go awry.

For many years the response process has been heavily tilted toward business reply cards and envelopes. Now, telephone calls to toll-free lines and Internet responses generate significant amounts of traffic.

Sample business reply envelope. (Courtesy Wyers Direct)

When planning a response management system, a reasonable first step is to compile a response database. Ranges of options are appropriate for differing circumstances such as:

• **Capturing responses from scratch.** This unsophisticated system requires data entry personnel to enter the full name, address, and other pertinent information on the reply device. In almost every case, this is a poor use of your database and is subject to lots of data entry errors.

- **Unique identification number.** Using a unique identification number saves both money and data entry time while vastly improving information accuracy.

Unique identifier—"finder number." (Courtesy Innovative Graphics)

Unique identifying numbers—sometimes referred to as "finder numbers"—should be placed somewhere on each record and on the BRC, if there is one. Upon receipt of the response, only this number is required for entry and the appropriate record automatically is called up.

- **Bar codes.** If your goal is to remove all initial keying activity upon receipt of the response, print a barcode on the BRC. To fulfill the request, scanners automatically will read the unique identification number and retrieve the record.

- **OCR readers.** With the advent of affordable processing power and sophisticated OCR (optical character recognition) software, fully automated response systems are becoming commonplace for some applications. If properly executed, these OCR-based systems allow the response forms to be automatically scanned, completely eliminating manual data entry. Then, fulfillment activities can begin with as little human intervention as possible.

Tech Tip

It's important to choose unique number strings carefully. They must be unique, not too long (creating the possibility of more input errors) and should not be a direct representation of anything the recipient might perceive as being confidential—i.e., telephone number, social security number, date of birth, etc.

Sample personalized reply device. (Courtesy Wyers Direct)

Response Analysis

As requests are fulfilled, all captured responses should be tabulated and analyzed. This is the point at which direct response advertising differs from traditional advertising. Here, the direct marketer begins to review the specific results of the specific mailing and overall campaign. Tabulating overall response rates and calculating "cost per response" figures are necessary to determine effectiveness and profitability.

After analyzing many campaigns, direct marketers can create mathematical models that anticipate response, cost per response, and financial return, all things being equal. This principle is at the core of the direct marketing field, regardless of marketing vehicle used. Payback is easy to determine. Whether you're analyzing a single mailing or a multiyear campaign, tally all costs associated with the outbound mailing including list acquisition, creative, production, and postal costs. Next, calculate gross inflow of revenues. Then, subtract all response costs including variable labor, cost of goods sold, fulfillment, and allocation to overhead. Lastly, do the math.

An appealing aspect of direct mail is that cost per response can be positively identified, unlike many competing mass-market advertising vehicles. Based on what the numbers say, determine your next step. If subsequent mailings are appropriate, the numbers will tell you. Regardless of whether you're satisfied with your return, start testing your mail components as opposed to your previous best pulling piece.

PAL POINT... Test everything. Please refer to Chapter 11 and plan testing into your program. Allow no sacred cows. Test the envelope, creative, headlines, fonts, inserts, shapes, printing, colours, everything. Each time take the response and compare it to the best performing piece in your arsenal. Perhaps one of the best things about the direct mail and direct response industry is that the numbers don't lie. Over time, you will become armed with the vital information you need to drive exceptional marketing performance in the future. Good luck, wherever you are in your quest for direct response excellence.

50 Electronic Updates: The Wave of the Future

Wouldn't it be easy for clients if their mailing services partners offered daily electronic job status updates on large-volume jobs? Wouldn't a lot of time-wasting telephone tag be avoided? More and more letter shops think so. Although the direct mail industry hasn't yet reached the FedEx standard for information on demand, this day may not be far away.

In our detail-oriented direct mail industry, accurate and timely information is critically important. Project success depends on gathering the right information and making the right decisions. During the 1990s, a lot of people decreased their telephone usage in favor of email, but communication still originated when customers made inquiries. The best suppliers proactively provided customers with status updates as best they could, but without automated systems, problems still fell through the cracks.

Fast forward to today. Technology has blazed new trails that make mailing customers' lives easier. Progressive high-volume letter shops now offer their clients current job status via email before the working day starts. Typical information includes inventory and production rate data, as well as benchmark goals.

Core Benefits of an Electronic Update System

- **Inventory.** Assume you're working on a million-piece mailing with a dozen different components for a client. If an email inventory status arrives each morning, you'll immediately know if you should be concerned about any aspect of the job. What if your daily report shows that the letter shop received 250,000 each of four different coloured envelopes yesterday? What if you need 500,000 blue envelopes? Instantly, you'd know you have a problem on your hands.

Without the update, it's likely you wouldn't have learned of this situation until later on—and possibly too late to do anything about it.

- **Delivery dates.** Electronic information updating systems allow you to carefully monitor your production counts. Assume you've promised your customer an eight-day turn-around time on a million-piece mailing. If your production department averages 100,000 pieces on each of the first four days, you can and should ask how the deadline will be met. Again, under the old information paradigm, you may not discover this situation until it's too late to do anything. Now, with daily electronic updates, you're armed with enough information to ask the right questions and let your customers know you have a potential problem on your hands, if it gets to that.

- **Benchmarking.** Production counts by themselves are good, but not good enough. The best daily electronic status update systems also include production benchmarks. If your morning email shows that your lettershop has planned to produce 100,000 pieces on each of the first six production days, and 200,000 on days seven and eight, then you'll know that you're right on schedule. In short, this information will help remove your running around.

PAL POINT... It's a waste of time to ask for data that should be supplied to you in the first place. In this day and age, information should literally be at your fingertips so you have more time to focus on what's truly important—making informed decisions. Is the mailing services industry operating at the FedEx standard yet? Unfortunately, the answer is "no." However, some leading companies have their eye on completely auto-mated systems that allow customers to retrieve information on secure sites whenever they want. As an industry, we're not there yet...but just wait.

APPENDICES

Appendix 1:
General Questions for a
Typical Direct Mail Campaign

1. Mailing quantity _____

2. Frequency _____

3. Type: ❏ Lettermail (1st)   ❏ Publications Mail (2nd)
   ❏ Addressed Admail (3rd)

4. Envelope: ❏ Yes   ❏ No (if no, skip to #10)

5. What size is the envelope?   ❏ #10, Business
   ❏ 5⅞×9 in.   ❏ 9×12 in.   ❏ Other _____

6. Is envelope a window?   ❏ Yes   ❏ No

7. How many inserts?

   #1: _____

   #2: _____

   #3: _____

   #4: _____

   #5: _____

   #6: _____

8. Which insert is addressed? _____

9. Size of address piece _____

10. Is it a self-mailer?
   ❏ Self-mailer Size: Folded: _____ Flat: _____
   ❏ Newsletter Size: Folded: _____ Flat: _____
   ❏ Magazine Size: Folded: _____ Flat: _____
   ❏ Postcard Size: _____
   ❏ Other Size: _____

11. Is there an indicia? ❏ Yes   ❏ No, metering   ❏ No, stamp

12. Is clip sealing required? ❏ Yes _____ how many   ❏ No

13. How is it addressed?
    ❏ Cheshire Label   ❏ Inkjet   ❏ Laser
    ❏ Other _____

14. Is data manipulation required? ❏ Yes   ❏ No

15. How many files? _____   ❏ Tapes   ❏ Diskettes
    ❏ CD   ❏ Other _____

16. Are there different mail pieces (splits)? ❏ Yes   ❏ No

17. Address Accuracy   ❏ No   ❏ Yes   ❏ …and Correction

18. Is there just a name and address, or is there a client code,
    VIN #, etc.? _____

19. Are there any special reports that are required?

    _____

    _____

    _____

    _____

Notes:
- If a mailing is metered, postage money should be
  required before production begins, since meters
  need to be replenished.
- If approvals are required, please note in the job
  specifications.
- Nonstandard data reports can be generated. There
  are fees for each, and they take time to perform.
  Advance notification is important.
- Uppercase/lowercase conversion is possible, although
  it is not 100% accurate. For example, some names
  like "MacArthur" may result in "Macarthur."
- Even small data projects require an ample amount of
  time to set up; therefore expect minimum charges.

Appendix 2:
Sample Job Checklist

Client/Job _____ Job No. _____

❏ Sales notified   Date _____

❏ Quote sent   Date _____

❏ Mail date established   Date _____

❏ Schedule completed   Date _____

❏ Tape disposition   Date _____

❏ Material disposition   Date _____

❏ Job confirmation sent   Date _____

❏ Signed job confirmation received   Date _____

❏ Tapes/files received   Date _____

❏ Postal permit   Date _____

❏ Drop-ship required   Date _____

❏ BMC/SCF report received   Date _____

❏ Drop-ship spreadsheet created   Date _____

Data Processing
❏ Convert sheet submitted   Date _____

❏ Group I sheet submitted   Date _____

❏ NCOA acknowledgment sent   Date _____

❏ Merge/purge sheet sent   Date _____

❏ Order for match mailing checked   Date _____

❏ I have reviewed the convert   Date _____

❏ I have reviewed the presort   Date _____

❏ I have checked the presort report for proper containerization/palletization   Date _____

❏ Postage request sent   Date _____

❏ Samples have been printed/run   Date _____

Laser

❏ I have a signed proof letter   Date _____

❏ Quality checkpoint sheet submitted to Data Processing   Date _____

Material

❏ All delivery receipts double-checked   Date _____

❏ Quantity received sufficient for job + spoilage   Date _____

❏ Inventory spreadsheet created   Date _____

Mail Plant

❏ Postage received

❏ Sample board and/or set-up samples submitted   Date _____

❏ I have approved, signed-off samples   Date _____

❏ I have/am receiving production QC samples   Date _____

❏ Daily production spreadsheet created   Date _____

❏ Samples have been sent   Date _____

❏ Spreadsheets are being updated daily   Date _____

❏ Spoilage is being kept and scanned daily   Date _____

Job complete: Date _____

Job billed: Date _____

Appendix 3:
Sample List of Required Information

All accounts must have the following information assembled into a file or notebook.

Basic Account Information
- Internal contacts (names, phone numbers, fax numbers, addresses, home phone numbers)
- External contacts (names, phone numbers, fax numbers, addresses, home phone numbers)
- Store/market/versions
- Numbers
- Addresses—hard copy and PC- or mainframe-compatible media
- Overview of client purpose/history
- Overview of job process
- Pricing
- Billing

Details of Job Processing
- Typical job steps, program names, flow charts, expected input tapes
- Area for potential problems
- Verification/quality control checkpoints
- Previous problems and solutions

Reports/Output
- Report names, program names, when to run, samples
- Report distribution
- Verification of reports

Documentation

- Copies of tables—hard copy and PC or mainframe compatible
- Sample run sheets from job setup
- Sample special forms or requests
- Sample mailing pieces

Appendix 4:
Sample Quality Checkpoints Form

Use this form in conjunction with the live laser sign-off approval submitted to your Data Processing department for laser imaging. This form should note specific characteristics of the form and copy like the following: "If XX copy is used in the Johnson box, body copy in paragraph two should read XX" or "if address is in Texas, then home logo must appear at bottom right of form," etc.

Once this form is completed, attach a live laser sign-off.

Quality Checkpoints

Client/job _____

Job no _____

Date submitted _____ / _____ / _____

(Use yellow marker on live laser to highlight checkpoints and circled numbers to identify location of checkpoints.)

Form _____

Font _____

Copy _____

Unique elements _____

Colour _____

Size/shape _____

List/geography _____

Must get right _____

Required sign-offs _____

Appendix 5: Incoming File Preparation

Develop internal policies that you need in order to effectively process incoming files. This means listing all media that you can accept, and keeping it current. Also, make sure your storage procedures are written so that no customer data is ever lost or misplaced.

Sample Data Policies

1. All incoming customer tapes, disks, cartridges, etc., will be kept in our tape library and unless clients specifically request the return of their media, they will be deleted after 90 days. It is extremely important to make the customer aware of this policy. Be sure it is on every quote and confirmation.

2. A record layout and estimated quantity must accompany each and every file we receive, including email files. Remember the record layout is our road map to what is on the file or tape. Without it we don't have enough information to proceed. Our clients do not need to guess about record layout.

Sample List of Acceptable Media

Account managers for direct mail services companies should know exactly what file formats and media types are acceptable to their data processing department. A sample list may look like the following:

- IBM 3480 cartridges, compressed or uncompressed
- IBM 3490E cartridges
- Mag tapes (reel/round tapes)—1,600 or 6,250 EBCDIC or ASCII
- IBM/PC-compatible data
- ZIP disks

- Diskettes—write-protect all diskettes;
  use Excel to test for readability
- CD-ROM
- Electronic transmission—email, Internet, FTP

Converting Files

Many computer systems have certain programs that are used over and over again. Your mailer may repeatedly use presort, list hygiene, and merge/purge programs. These programs are set up to look for specific data—such as last name or street address—in a specific place on every tape.

If a tape has not been converted to a "standard format," that data may not be in that specific place and the program may not produce accurate output. Therefore, data processing departments need to convert each tape to a common format so their programs know where to look for each specific piece of data.

Record Layout

A record layout is essentially a "map" of what is on a file or tape. It shows the location of data within each record, which must be in the same place in each record. It shows the length of each field and the type of data (alpha or numeric). Every file or tape received must be accompanied by a complete and accurate record layout. Files shouldn't be converted without one, and good mail shops have a "no exceptions" allowed policy.

There is no more important part of any job than converting the file. If this is done incorrectly, the entire job will be wrong. What's worse, it may not be immediately apparent that an error was made. It is important to be very careful when giving data processing conversion instructions.

Information must be exact. All other stages of a job will be based upon what has been converted and where it was placed afterward.

What to Convert

It is essential that direct mail account managers understand what their customers are trying to accomplish in order to properly instruct the data processing department on what to convert. They need to be clear about what data will be used and how it will be used. Don't forget about how this data might be used for result tabulation. Will there be codes to capture? Should there be an account number? How about a match code or barcode? Again, be fully aware of how the data will be used in order to convert a file properly.

Personalization

If you need to create laser-imaged letters, be sure to get clear instructions on how the salutation and address area should look. Should the salutation be Dear Mary Jones, Dear Ms. Jones, or Dear Mary? Is there a salutation field in the file? Will your data processing department need to isolate the first and last names to make the salutation? Is there a title field? Should the job be run through the gender-assign program?

Sort Order Is Important!

If a job is to be run multiple-up, the data must be processed in an appropriate order. "East/west" imaging (first name left, next name right, etc.) will cause problems because the stacks will be out of order after final trimming. Instead, "north/south" ordering allows jobs to be processed, separated, and married with the job ending up in proper mailing sequence.

Appendix 6:
De-Dupe Merge/Purge Form

EXPECTED RECORDS AFTER DEDUPE

	TAPE#	CODE	DESCRIPTION	QUANTITY	
				INPUT	POST-CONVERT
KILL					
1.					
2.					
3.					
4.					
5.					
6.					
7.					
8.					

Courtesy Direct Marketing Associates, Inc.

Appendix 7:
Merge/Purge and Data Manipulation
Questions and Answers

Merge/purge is so important to reducing postal costs that it deserves additional mention. Here are some commonly asked questions and answers about this vital data processing service.

Q: What is a merge/purge?
A: Merge/purge is the technique used to combine names, addresses, and related data from various mailing lists to identify and potentially eliminate duplicate names for a single mailing or to create a marketing database.

Q: Are all merge/purges pretty much alike?
A: Actually, they're not. The merge/purge from one service bureau (or in-house computer service department) to another has differences.

A good merge/purge will:

- Save money.
- Provide you with control over the definition of what constitutes a "duplicate."
- Eliminate "real" duplicates yet not eliminate names you want to mail to (causing an "overkill" situation).
- Identify multiple buyers within an organization.
- Handle "eliminate," "suppress," and "fraud" files.
- Improve the printed appearance of the names and addresses.
- Give all the reports and statistics that direct marketers need for dealing effectively with list brokers and managers and making good future decisions to increase mail effectiveness.

- Prioritize lists.
- Be completed correctly and on time.

A superior merge/purge will also:

- Process all North American data instead of being country-specific.
- Increase response rates.
- Be both parameter-driven and flexible enough to meet all data needs.
- Carry all the information throughout the merge for future use.
- Provide reports showing examples of records that were dropped from the merge/purge.
- Allow customers to change data parameters after the merge/purge has been completed.

Q: Isn't there more to merge/purge? Specifically, what else should be looked for? What are the subtle differences?
A: Look for a data services company whose merge/purge programs can perform these "miracles" during processing:

- Use different criteria for determining duplication between business and consumer records.
- Correctly de-dupe records such as "IBM," "International Business Machines," and "Int'l/Bus Mach," for example.
- Use multiple techniques of matching during processing. For processing efficiency, some records are "exact matches" and others require more sophisticated algorithms.
- Search for duplicates with phonetic equivalency, similar spellings, common data entry errors, and transpositions. It should also have the capability to search within a postal code, a region, a state/province, or country for duplicates.

- Assign a male or female code to a record based on first names, exempting certain names like "Pat" or "Robin."
- Generate a city and state from a postal code.
- Link business firms throughout the nation.

Q: I don't know which merge/purge features are important for my file. How can I be sure?

A: The best way is to ask your direct mailing services partner for a printout of at least 5,000 records from your data file in a four-up Cheshire format, with name, title, company, division, address, city, province, and postal code code printed on the labels. Examine it. Look for duplicates. Get a general idea of what's on your data file and then ask for recommendations as to how to handle particular challenges such as:

- What is the best technique for determining duplicates for this file?
- How should address components be separated and identified?
- What techniques should be used to identify businesses, professions, institutions, etc.?
- How should marginal (possible) duplicates be identified? Then, what procedures should be implemented to make the best decisions?

Q: What are the different kinds of systems and other methods of identifying duplicates or possible duplicates?

A: The techniques used in North America (U.S. and Canada) to identify duplicates and possible duplicates include these:

- Mathematical equivalency
- Phonetic matching
- Multiple duplicate search
- Address patterning
- Unique business file patterning

- Linkage of firms throughout the nation
- Flexible matching criteria
- Identification of "possible" duplicates

Q: I've heard of a "match code" system. What is it used for?
A: Match codes, which are still used by many systems, were used by the first merge/purge systems as a standardized, simplified method of purging "exact" duplicates. This system takes a portion of each major field (such as the first three consonants of a last name, the first three letters of a street name and street number, and your postal code) and assigns this as your match code.

This method is adequate in many applications. However, the art and science of duplicate and possible duplicate identification has developed so that it includes other techniques of finding the duplication possibilities within a file or between multiple files.

Match code systems are still adequate to de-dupe many exact matches where the name and all address components are exactly alike. However, if there's not an exact match, name and address processing programs can have features that search for "maybe" matches. This is accomplished by determining how closely the various components of name and address records have to match for them to be considered duplicates.

Q: What is a "maybe" match?
A: Assume two records are electronically compared and found to be 98% alike. Are they duplicates? Probably. What if they are only 75% alike? Are they still duplicates? Maybe yes, maybe no. Provide maybe match instructions to your mailing services company. If you aren't sure what it should be in your case, ask for advice.

Q: What are two primary variable matching techniques?
A: Variable matching techniques come in two main categories. The first is the "point scoring" method in which elements are assigned numerical values. A second is the "dial" method whereby parameters or values are set in the program. This second approach compares similarities and differences in key parts of the record and determines the percentage or degree of match between one or more names and address records.

Both of these methods determine duplicate records based on their "conclusions." In addition to checking records in the same postal code or town, they can be set to compare records in BMC districts, states, or provinces.

Q: How important is it for a computer service bureau or in-house data processing department to edit the data provided to them from another computer house for a merge/purge?
A: Don't assume that the data provided to you has had the proper merge/purge processes done to meet your data requirements. Most companies involved with the capture, manipulation, and transference of data have different needs and use formats suitable to their own purposes.

The merge/purge software that your service bureau or in-house data processing department uses should provide extensive editing capabilities to determine the accuracy of the provided data prior to the merge/purge. This crucial step adds discipline to the file and ultimately determines the final success of the merge/purge process. Some of the editing of data that should be done include:

- Street name standardization and spelling correction
- City name spelling correction
- Postal code validation, assignment, and correction
- Title code and job title standardization
- Identification of company names

When choosing a service bureau or software vendor for your in-house data processing department, determine the degree and type of data editing that should be performed before each file is submitted for the final merge/purge or to a database assembling process.

Q: What are the different techniques used by a computer service bureau to determine which lists get credit for duplicate records?
A: There are five main ways of determining which list receives credit and thus payment for duplicate names in a merge/purge of multiple mailing lists. These are as follows:

- *Intentional priority ranking*—ranking by financial, relational, or subjective criteria

- *Random approach*—provides posting "credit" using a technique of first one and then the other list

- *Combination priority and random*—the first few lists are ranked in a priority with all remaining lists receiving random allocation

- *Priority random groupings*—priority groups of lists with random allocation within these groups

- *Matrix data retention*—database construction in which the multiple source and pertinent information can be retained in a file

Q: How do I determine the priority in which the lists should be ranked?
A: There are many ways to determine list priority. Two common ones are:

- *Financial motivation*—such as best net name deal, lowest cost list, etc. In general, the lower the cost of the list or the lower the net name guarantee, the higher the list should be placed in the ranking order

- *Relational motivation*—including business, organizational, and/or personal relationships. These factors could be considered in ranking priority. For example, a list owner who is also the list broker could and probably would choose to place his or her list in a more highly ranked position

Q: What is the difference between a business merge/purge and a consumer merge/purge?

A: There are two primary types of merge/purges:

- Business/institutional
- Consumer/household

To accommodate business marketers, some data service bureaus and list generation companies merely apply business functions to their already created consumer merge/purge software. However, some companies offer a series of distinct programs designed especially for the business-to-business merge/purge.

Business files are more complex and include more fields of information such as company name, job title, department name, etc., all of which are used on the addressing record. On the other hand, consumer files typically only image basic name and address information. Business merge/purge software must be designed to look at the additional fields in order to identify and kill true duplicates and undeliverable records.

Q: What is business chaining and how could it help my mailing?

A: Business chaining is an option your data services provider should offer if you intend on processing a business merge/purge. This process links multiple records within a corporation. Since no records are eliminated, just linked together in a logical manner, you have control as to how many employees per company you wish to mail to.

Q: People advise me that I should test different variables. Can data service providers do this for me? Why should it be done?

A: When working on a direct response marketing program, test different variables to see exactly which ones bring in the highest response rate. Certain lists or list segments will generate higher levels of response. You need to know which ones do. In addition, you need to test various creative elements including envelopes, postage (stamps vs. meter), copy, graphics, etc. You will want to analyze different variables against a control package so you can better target your mailings in the future.

Good data service providers have developed computer software that can split your "test" names and apply different key codes to each list being tested.

Q: Please explain Canada Post Corporation (CPC) postal presorting. How can it save me money?

A: Postal presorting is the categorizing of data records into different levels of cost-based specifications designed by CPC. The basic principle involved is that postal discounts are offered for activities that lower CPC mail delivery costs. In general, the more automation-friendly or geographically concentrated your mailing is, the lower your postal costs.

If you take advantage of postal discounts, your mailing services company should provide the Post Office with reports that indicate the quantity of pieces that qualify for each level of discount.

Q: What type of statistics should I get from my merge/purge?

A: Good data services companies will automatically provide you with summary statistics from the output of the merge/purge. This report should tell you the quantity of "inter" and "intra" duplicates for each list included in your merge. It should also provide a listing of the quantity and type of errors for each list. Reports customized to your particular needs should also be made available. An additional report should be made available that shows how many records could not be processed as a result of incorrect postal codes, incomplete addresses, and inaccurate city names, etc.

When you analyze your reports, you should get a good idea of the lists that will work for you. If there is a high duplication rate between your "house" file, if you have one, and other lists, you can be more assured that the people on the outside file are interested in your content and conclude that this list should work well.

Q: How do I get samples to compare different data service providers? Can I get a test done on my file? How much does this cost?
A: This is another good way to tell the difference between service bureaus. Reputable mailing services companies will do tests on a portion of your file at no charge.

Q: What are some differences between USPS and CPC postal systems that your mailing services companies need to be aware of?
A: Canada has a number of unique features to the addressing and postal code systems. Included are:

- The grid system of house and apartment numbering in the western provinces
- The similarity of French language street names (particularly in Quebec and New Brunswick)
- French direction code abbreviations. For example, "O" is the French abbreviation for "W" (West).

It is mandatory that your data service professionals understand these differences during merge/purge.

The Canadian postal coding system is an alphanumeric system, whereas the United States zip code system is numeric only. Both countries are constantly adding, changing, and deleting individual postal codes. Your service bureau must be aware of this and update its software accordingly. In addition, CPC requires mail to be prepared in National Distribution Guide sequence in order to qualify for even the highest level of third-class postage.

Your high-volume mailing services provider should also be able to presort your data and assign Canadian letter carrier presort codes. If the density of your mailing doesn't warrant postal presorting services, your data services should be able to commingle your mail with other mailings to lower your postal costs.

Q: Since I can't judge merge/purge by price alone, how can I be sure that I am dealing with a good data services company?

A: Choose your computer service bureau the same way you would pick any new employee—interview leading candidates and ask for references. If you like what you hear, you should be more comfortable with your first choice.

Appendix 8:
Sample Merge/Purge Report Fields

Merge/Purge Reports

Become familiar with merge/purge reports. It is very important to double-check the output quantity, ensure that the purge file was used correctly, verify the priority of the lists, and review a reasonable sampling of some of the duplicate records.

Explanation of Merge/Purge Reports

Column 1—FILE CODE: Each should have a FILE CODE that distinguishes it for the other files in the merge/purge. This allows separation of the files after the de-duping process to make selections.

Column 2—PRIORITY: Each file in the merge/purge is given a priority. If a duplicate record is found, it will drop from the file with the lower priority.

Column 3—DESCRIPTION: Identifies each input file.

Column 4—INPUT: The input quantity for each file.

Column 5—PRG-DROP: The number of records that drop from each file, resulting from a match to the purge file.

Column 6—MLT-DROP: The number of records that drop because they appear on more than one file (duplicates that occur between files).

Column 7—SNG-DROP: The number of records that drop because they appear on one file more than once (duplicates that occur within the same file).

Column 8—SNG-BUYER: The number of records SAVED from each file that ONLY appeared on one input file.

Column 9—MLT-BUYER: The number of records SAVED from each file that appeared on more than one input file.

Column 10—OUTPUT: The total number of records saved from each file.

Column 11—PCT KEPT: The percentage of records that were saved from each file.

Appendix 9:
Barcode Standards

When using barcodes, be sure that both tabletop and hand-held scanners can read them. Test them on both pieces of equipment. Also, verify the information after it has been read. A common barcode mailing piece identification sequence standard is as follows:

- First 5 digits—job number
- Next 2 digits—cell/lot/version number
- Next 7 digits—unique sequence number

Once the live sign-off has been approved, give a sample of the piece to a supervisor. This sample should indicate which barcode should be scanned (if more than one) and show the difference between versions, lots, and cells.

Next, these scanned records should be given on a daily basis to the data processing department. The downloaded quantity should be recorded and checked daily to determine if the number of scanned records seems logical (i.e., you saw a lot of spoilage but only saw 100 recorded in the downloaded file). Then, each week determine if you need to perform the match and reprint the pieces.

Be sure that 100% mailing instructions appear in all tasks, including data processing, addressing, bindery, inserting, and hand work (hand section does the scanning).

Appendix 10:
Image Proofing Procedural Standards

Use this checklist to ensure that you have reviewed all possible areas for errors and/or omissions. Watch carefully for:

- Misused words such as "you're" and "your"
- Grammatical errors
- Address positioning errors; cut the form down and put into an actual envelope and do the "tap" test
- Gender match (male name with Mr., female name with Ms.)
- Incorrect initial first name fields
- Default names
- Data table errors

Also, be sure to have a dump of the unconverted records you are using as sign-offs to double-check that data has not changed or been altered during the DP process.

Live Laser Sign-Off Checklist

Endorsement line
- ❏ On all records
- ❏ Only on AUTOCR records
- ❏ Not required

Keyline
- ❏ Customer codes*
- ❏ Sequence no.**
- ❏ Truck/pallet/tray no.

Name and address
- ❏ U/L case
- ❏ Mr. & Mrs.

- ❏ Default title
- ❏ Postal and walk codes
- ❏ All address lines present
- ❏ Shows thru window

Salutation
- ❏ P/U last name/ first name only
- ❏ Default/special salutation
- ❏ Punctuation
- ❏ U/L case
- ❏ Initial only

Body copy/reply

❏ Variable text

❏ Line wraps

❏ Copy on reverse

❏ Form code

❏ Position of copy

❏ $ upgrades calculated OK

❏ Min/max $ $ OK

❏ Rounding correct

Converting samples

❏ Trim OK

❏ Fold OK

❏ Address shows through window

❏ Customer sign-off

❏ Special cells

Verify that codes are accurate by counting the number of digits, correct alpha/numeric combination, starting numbers, and comparing to a dump of unconverted record.
**Be sure sequence numbers are printed as required. Is it on every record, every 100th, etc.?

Appendix 11: Lettershop Procedures

Success in the lettershop depends on developing good procedures and following them.

Suggested Guidelines

Account managers should prepare complete samples of each version of every job and distribute them appropriately. A good rule of thumb is not to allow any job to begin unless the account manager has provided these samples. All materials should be put in inserting order.

Then, production samples should be pulled several times a day from each producing department and thoroughly examined. Critical things to look for include accurate fold, window position, insertion order, correct material, and version. If there isn't a procedure in place to get these production samples, one should be started. This applies to bindery, addressing, inserting, and saddle stitching.

Account managers should take a few moments several times a day to walk through the area of the plant where their jobs are being processed. Do spot pulls from several machines, look at completed pieces, check the addressing for position, correct information, etc. You may be able to spot a problem before it becomes too serious.

Postal Permits

When working on mailing projects for new customers, be sure to ask if they have their own permits or if they will be using yours. If they have their own, be sure the designated point of entry is suitably located. Sometimes you may have to open a permit for a customer.

These are some examples of indicias. Always have a CPC tech review all new permits before they're used in live production.

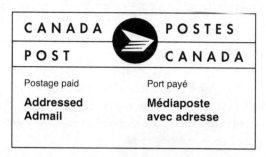

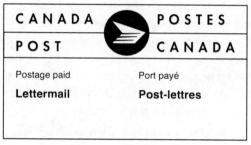

Note: *The mailer's permit number must be added to the bottom portion of the box.*

Appendix 12:
An Overs Guide for Specialty Finishing

Please note: The following table should only be used as a guideline for spoilage. Adherence does not necessarily guarantee that a particular project will not be short.

Variables that affect spoilage include the following:

- Temperature and humidity extremes affect equipment, paper, and glue.
- Extreme stock weights—either very heavy or light—are difficult to work with.
- Various varnishes and other paper coatings react differently to different glues and applications.
- Small-quantity projects require a higher percentage of overs compared to large-quantity projects because makeready spoilage is distributed over fewer pieces.
- Multiple code changes and lots increase spoilage requirements. On multiple-code projects, makeready sheets should come from one code. Samples should be provided for each code and be well marked when shipped.

Every project is unique and has its own characteristics. The following guidelines can be used to reduce shortages. However, we do recommend verifying the required overs on every specialty finishing project.

Specialty Finishing Spoilage Guidelines

Job Description	Required Extra Sheets		
	Makeready	Tune-up	Live Run
Basic folding with glue	500	500	1%

Example: Four-page folder tipped shut with fugitive glue

Difficult folding with glue	2,000	500	3%

Example: Form diecut pocket, three rollfolds and double-gate on 100-lb. coated stock

Basic mailer with glue	500	500	3%

Example: One remoistenable-glue strip, two perfs, and fold in half

Difficult mailer with pattern glue	2,000	500	10%

Example: 1-in.-wide glue strip, two perfs, one time perf, formed pocket with $1/2$-in. short rollfolds on 50-lb. stock

High-level custom-designed	5,000	1,000	10%

Example: Hot-melt U-shaped glue, time cutting, second remoistenable-glue strip, pocket-glue to create BRC inside zipper perf

Inkjet imaging	500	100	1%

Example: Four 8-line address

Appendix 13: Addressed Admail Definition

Beginning on March 1, 1999, the Addressed Admail definition became:

Mailable items, bearing a uniform message, that promote the sale or use of products or services; report on financial performance, primarily for promotional purposes; or solicit donations or contributions.

With this new definition, Addressed Admail became solely an advertising and promotional product. As such, mailings containing non-promotional material are not acceptable as Addressed Admail.

Prior to March 1, 1999, the wording for all pieces in an Addressed Admail mailing had to be identical, and only the address block could be personalized.

Effective March 1, 1999, the wording of Addressed Admail pieces no longer needed be identical. Advertisers were now able to fully personalize their promotional messages by tailoring the entire content of the piece to the recipient. To qualify as Addressed Admail, however, pieces must meet the following criteria:

1. The intent of the mailing must be promotional. *The intent of the mailing must be to motivate an individual to buy or acquire a product or service, or to contribute to or support a cause.*

2. The theme of the mailing must be uniform. *The mail items must have the same specific purpose and the same specific goal.*

As you have read in the new Addressed Admail definition, all pieces must now be promotional in nature. To determine whether your pieces qualify as Addressed Admail, it will be important for you to understand the difference between a promotional and a nonpromotional piece.

Remember: If you are part of the vast majority of Addressed Admail customers who already mail promotional items, the definition change will not affect you. However, you might want to take advantage of some of the additional benefits the new definition offers.

To determine whether a mail piece is promotional, you must ask the question, "What is the intent of the piece?"

If the intent is to motivate an individual to buy or acquire a product or service, or to contribute to or support a cause, it is promotional and therefore acceptable as Addressed Admail.

Appendix 14:
CPC Addressed Admail Service Standards

CPC Addressed Admail service standards are:

- Local Municipality: 3 business days
- In Province: 4–5 business days
- National: 4–15 business days

An additional day may be added to the service standards for the delivery of Dimensional Addressed Admail.

Please note:

- The number of days excludes the day of induction to CPC, weekends, and statutory holidays.

- Weekend and statutory holiday deposits are considered deposited on the following business day.

- These service standards do not apply to Northern Regions and Remote Centres as defined by Canada Post, or to redirected or returned Items.

- Service standards are subject to change without notice.

Three-day delivery windows exist within these provincial and national standards for Addressed Admail mailings inducted in specific urban centres for delivery in other urban centres. The three-day range varies by the geographic locations of mail induction and delivery destinations.

With planning in association with CPC delivery standards can be further fine-tuned, but are not exact due to the nature of the Addressed Admail Product.

Note: *Postal information is provided as a courtesy and should be used as a guideline only. Mailers must have all mail pieces reviewed and approved by their CPC representative or lettershop CPC liaison. No responsibility or liability shall be assumed by the authors or the publisher for changes in specifications or typographical errors in these charts.*

Appendix 15:
CPC Lettermail Specifications
as of April 2006

	Length		Width		Thickness		Weight	
	Min. (mm)	Max. (mm)	Min. (mm)	Max. (mm)	Min. (mm)	Max. (mm)	Min. (g)	Max. (g)
Standard								
Envelope	140	245	90	156	0.18	5	3	50
Self-Mailer	140	245	90	156	0.18	5	5	50
Card or Postcard**	140	235	90	120	0.18	**	**	**
Nonstandard Oversize								
Envelope	140	380	90	270	0.5	20	10	500
Card or Postcard**	N/A	380	N/A	270	N/A	20	N/A	N/A

** No specific weight requirements for cards—dependent upon grammage of paper used and the size of the card.

Note: Postal information is provided as a courtesy and should be used as a guideline only. Mailers must have all mail pieces reviewed and approved by their CPC representative or lettershop CPC liaison. No responsibility or liability shall be assumed by the authors or the publisher for changes in specifications or typographical errors in these charts.

Appendix 16:
CPC Admail Specifications
as of April 2006

Category	Length	Width	Thick-ness	Weight
Short and Long Machineable	max. 245 mm min. 100 mm	156 mm 90 mm	5 mm 0.18 mm	50 g 3 g
Postcards or Cards Machineable	max. 235 mm min. 140 mm	120 mm 90 mm	5 mm 0.18 mm	50 g N/A
Oversize* Machineable	max. 380 mm min. 140 mm	270 mm 90 mm	20 mm 0.5 mm	500 g 10 g
Short and Long Presort (LCP and NDG)	max. 245 mm min. 100 mm	156 mm 70 mm	5 mm 0.18 mm	100 g N/A
Oversize* Presort (LCP and NDG)	max. 380 mm min. 100 mm	270 mm 70 mm	20 mm 0.18 mm	500 g N/A

*An item becomes oversize when it exceeds any one of the maximum dimensions and/or weight of short and long items.

Note: *Postal information is provided as a courtesy and should be used as a guideline only. Mailers must have all mail pieces reviewed and approved by their CPC representative or lettershop CPC liaison. No responsibility or liability shall be assumed by the authors or the publisher for changes in specifications or typographical errors in these charts.*

Appendix 17:
CPC Unaddressed Admail
Specifications as of April 2006

Letter Carrier Presort*

Category	Length	Width	Thick-ness	Weight
Residential Distribution	35.56 cm max.	15.24 cm max.	1.91 cm max.	230 g max.
Business Distribution	35.56 cm max.	25.4 cm max.	1.91 cm max.	230 g max.
Minimum	70 cm² area (10.85 sq. in.)		0.18 mm	N/A

Non-Letter Carrier Presort**

Category	Length	Width	Thick-ness	Weight
Residential & Business Distribution	35.56 cm	28 cm	3.81 cm	1,000 g
Samples	22.86 cm	15.24 cm	2.54 cm	500 g
Minimum	N/A	N/A	N/A	N/A

Please note that for mailings containing items weighing between 500 and 1,000 grams, the customer must schedule the mailing by contacting a Canada Post Representative.

* The delivery mode that falls under the specifications of Letter Carrier Routes is simply "LC" (for Letter Carrier).
** All other delivery modes, which include RR (rural routes), SS (suburban services), GD (general delivery), LB (lock boxes), CF (call for), MR (motorized routes), and DIR (directs) fall under the specifications for "Non-Letter Carrier Routes."

Note: *Postal information is provided as a courtesy and should be used as a guideline only. Mailers must have all mail pieces reviewed and approved by their CPC representative or lettershop CPC liaison. No responsibility or liability shall be assumed by the authors or the publisher for changes in specifications or typographical errors in these charts.*

Appendix 18:
Typical Material Management Guidelines

Receiving/Packaging Guidelines

This section contains important information about procedures that must be met and followed for materials being delivered.

- Carton labels
- Carton packaging
- Press sheets
- Packing slips/bills of lading
- Pallet requirements
- Stacking cartons on pallets

All material being delivered must be in cartons, except for press sheets.

Carton Labels

Two labels must be affixed to the outside of each carton on opposite sides with one label facing outward on the pallet. The following information must be on the label:

- Client
- Description of piece (outer envelope, BRE, brochure, letterhead, etc.)
- Code
- Quantity per bundle (except for envelopes and BREs)
- Quantity per carton
- Docket number if possible

Any other information on the label is OK, but the information above is mandatory.

Carton Packaging

All cartons should be filled to the top of each carton. Any excess space in between material should have packing paper.

- No carton should exceed the weight of 35 lb. (16 kg)
- A sample of the item must be taped or glued on the outside of each carton beside the carton label.
- All inserts must be equal quantities and must not exceed 4 in. (102 mm) in height.
- For self-mailers, the bundles must be banded two ways. (to make a cross).
- All inserts within the bundle must face the same way.

Press Sheets

- Can be delivered on any size pallet
- Cannot overhang the edge of the pallet
- Must be banded to the pallet to avoid movement of the material
- Must have a skid sheet with the following information:
    - ☞ Client name
    - ☞ Job name
    - ☞ Quantity of press sheets
    - ☞ How many singles per sheet
    - ☞ Total quantity of singles (e.g., 500 press sheets at 10-up equal 5,000 singles)

Packing Slips/Bills of Lading

A packing slip or bill of lading must arrive with the shipment. Either the driver is to have possession of the paperwork or it must be attached to the pallet that comes off first. (Courier bill not accepted.)

Include the following information on the packing slip:

- Client
- Job name
- Description of piece (outer envelope, BRE, lift-memo, letterhead, etc.)
- Code(s)
- Quantity per bundle (except for envelopes and BREs)
- Quantity per carton
- Quantity per code
- Total number of full cartons
- Total number of part cartons (must be on top of the pallet and clearly marked)
- Total quantity in shipment
- Total number of pallets
- Docket number if possible

Any other information on the packing slip is OK, but the information above is mandatory.

Pallet Requirements

The pallets on which your inserts are delivered (not press sheets) must meet these specific requirements.

- Pallets must measure 40×48 in. (1016×1219 mm)
- Total weight of the pallet must not exceed 2100 lb. (950 kg)
- Pallets must not be damaged
- Pallets must have three runners (2×4 in., 51×102 mm), running in the 48-in. direction
- Cartons must be securely wrapped to the pallet

Stacking Cartons on Pallets

The cartons in which your material is packed must meet the following requirements:

- Cartons must be stacked on pallets with the carton label and samples facing outward.
- Cartons cannot overhang over the edge of the pallet.
- Cartons that are part must be put on the top of the pallet.
- Cartons are to be cross-piled layer by layer; this will increase the stability factor.
- Each layer must have the same amount.

Sample Packaging Instructions

For best results, the following regulations should be followed. The correct codes must be used on the correct envelope and inserts and the pieces themselves must remain insertable.

1. Boxes should weigh less than 25 lb. (11.3 kg)
2. Boxes should consist of two or less layers
3. Pieces (samples) should be placed uniformly on end
4. Dividers are required between rows
5. Not to be packaged so that the samples/inserts curl
6. Not to be randomly packed into boxes
7. And all requirements as noted for shipping of general inserts noted previously

The amount of waste and the margin of error are directly related to how closely these instructions are followed. It goes without saying that there exists a significant negative correlation if they are not.

Appendix 19:
Managing Client Samples

Samples are required on most jobs. Check with your customer prior to creating your job order ticket to see what kind of samples they want—"live" or "Sample A" samples. Ask if they require samples of the laser and personalization only or samples of the entire package. How many samples do they want and at what production stage do they want them to be pulled from? Is there a special sample lot to produce samples from?

If "Sample A" sample packages are required, be sure to discuss this with your data center, include it in a production flowchart, and detail client-specific needs on the job order. If live records are required for the samples, again be sure to discuss with the data center and include detailed instructions on the order. Usually it's best to run all samples at the beginning of the job or at the beginning of each code or cell.

Sample requirements should be detailed on the job order form for the mail plant. Face-to-face discussions between account managers and plant supervisors are encouraged if the instructions are either complex or new. Actual trimmed and assembled pre-production sample packages are the best way to let everyone know what your customers expect.

Appendix 20:
Account Management Materials Handling Tips

Incoming Material

Get receiving tickets and samples of all incoming material. "Preflight" the job once all components are in. Included in this process is double-checking that all materials are the correct size and color, folds can be positioned properly, etc. Don't assume that since the correct sample is attached to the receipt, that the receipt reflects the correct inventory identification number. This can be very costly and time-consuming.

Receiving

Let your suppliers know your shipping hours, maximum pallet size, and any special requirements. For example, if you don't accept pallets that are stacked higher than 50 in. (1.27 m) or are unwrapped, say so.

If your continuous forms must be delivered upright, with one or two to a skid, let your suppliers know. If accepting rolls stacked poker chip style (laying down flat on their sides) causes production problems, don't accept them delivered this way.

Shipping/Outbound Material

All shipped material should be accompanied by a properly completed bill of lading (delivery ticket). Make sure the warehouse/logistics departments get a copy and that it includes:

- Client name, job name, and number
- Description of each piece
- Number of items including boxes, skids, trays, and overall quantity

- Exact delivery address with contact name and phone number
- Expected ship date and arrival date

In addition, a "pull ticket" should be created and sent to the warehouse for printing. This "pull ticket" notifies the warehouse personnel that they should take the material out of warehouse and stage it for shipping.

If you are shipping completed mail that mails from somewhere other than your facility, include a weight sticker with each pallet. Although the warehouse staff should do this task, the account manager still should make sure that each pallet is accounted for as it is placed on the outbound truck. Also, at this point account managers should perform an inventory on the excess material to check quantities. Be sure that material being returned makes sense after considering what was received and produced.

Excess or Leftover Material

Account managers should try to obtain excess material disposition instructions from customers prior to distributing the order. A reasonable policy is to destroy excess materials after 30 days unless specific instructions for disposition were received prior to beginning work on the job.

However, don't destroy any materials unless an actual sample of the piece is sent to the warehouse or some other department in charge of keeping production records. This means that when the warehouse is advised to destroy or recycle material, they will require not only written instructions and pull tickets, but they will also require an actual sample of the material to be destroyed. If there is similar material in house, characteristics that differentiate between the pieces should be clearly marked or indicated so that warehouse personnel will not have difficulty identifying the correct material.

Warehouse/logistics employees should participate in this procedure by saving a sample from each pallet being destroyed. Then, they can compare the sample piece provided, write a destroy date on each extracted piece, and return the dated pieces to the account managers once all material has been removed.

Billing Docket

Certain documents should be kept in dockets. These files are essential for QC maintenance and when jobs are run again they can be invaluable at assisting both the service company and the client by identifying problematic issues. Keeping these specific documents will support mailing claims, if they occur. Each docket must contain:

- Customer signed quote, job confirmation receipt, or purchase order
- Completed copy of internal job order
- Statements of mailing (SOM)
- LCP summary for each panel
- Discrepancy/shortage sheet (if needed)
- Any revised order or information
- Sample boards
- Ten or more samples verified by CPC
- Job activity report from mail software
- Disposition (excess material) sheet
- Error sheet (if needed)
- Transportation charges
- Each client should have established transportation rates and should be billed along with production and DP charges
- Postage billing codes

- When the docket comes from the accounting department, make sure that postage information has been
  detailed for you

Be sure to check the postage figures carefully and indicate
what to do with excess postage—pay down the invoice, put
into escrow, or send a refund check.

Appendix 21:
Fulfillment

Once responses to a direct mail program have been captured, all requests must be fulfilled. Some direct mail services companies offer fulfillment services to their clients. If you out-source your fulfillment requirements and you're interested in a single-source relationship with your mailer, make sure there's a good match between your needs and their fulfillment capabilities.

First, determine what type of fulfillment services you will need. Here are the three basic categories:

- *Information fulfillment*—collateral materials, tele-responses, more direct mail pieces, sales visits, etc.
- *Complementary product fulfillment*—supplying a product without any required payment
- *Paid product fulfillment*—supplying a product with a required payment

The process of fulfillment is a uniquely manual procedure that usually requires more attention and procedures than may appear at first glance. For example, fulfilling a dozen requests within an office environment is a simple, albeit time-consuming task. Fulfilling hundreds or thousands of requests is a logistics process few nonprofessionals are capable of completing without crossing many quality, insurance, and administrative hurdles.

If a product is being fulfilled, make sure that your fulfillment services provider has a clear understanding of your needs as well as how communication (verbal and digital) flows between client and vendor. An appropriate inventory tracking and control system is also necessary.

The timeliness of fulfilling requests is the basis by which organizations are measured. The timing will be evaluated based upon the expectations set within the original communication. Be sure if your original communication states "allow two weeks for delivery" that your processing, on average, will get it to them in one week.

Appendix 22:
Typical Grain Direction on Cut-Sheet Laser Printers

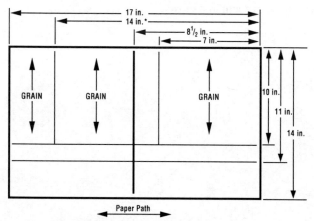

*Above 14 in. must be landscape, therefore must be 10 in. in width.

Appendix 23:
Form and Label Printing Orientation Coming Off Feed Rolls

For the proper printing and dispensing of forms and labels, please note the type and refer to the number for proper orientation.

❶

- Labels on outside of roll
- Printed across roll
- Top of label off first

❷

- Labels on outside of roll
- Printed across roll
- Bottom of label off first

❸

- Labels on outside of roll
- Printed with roll
- Right side off first

❹

- Labels on outside of roll
- Printed with roll
- Left side off first

❺

- Labels on inside of roll
- Printed across roll
- Top of label off first

❻

- Labels on inside of roll
- Printed across roll
- Bottom of label off first

❼

- Labels on inside of roll
- Printed with roll
- Right side off first

❽

- Labels on inside of roll
- Printed with roll
- Left side off first

Appendix 24:
Common Folding Diagrams

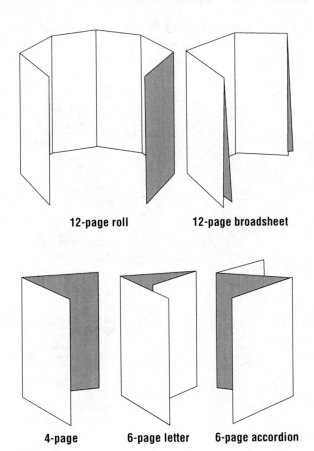

12-page roll   12-page broadsheet

4-page   6-page letter   6-page accordion

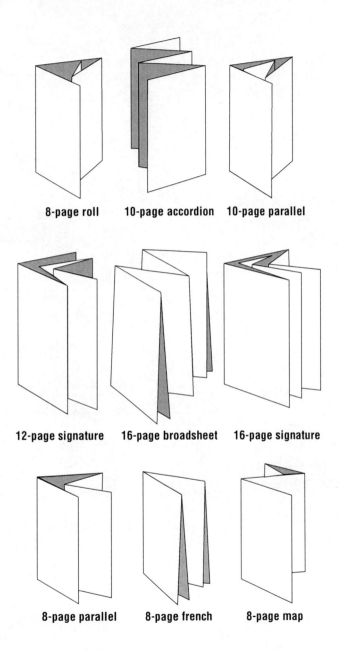

8-page roll   **10-page accordion**   **10-page parallel**

12-page signature   **16-page broadsheet**   **16-page signature**

8-page parallel   **8-page french**   **8-page map**

GLOSSARIES

Glossary 1—Data Terms

Active subscriber—A person or organization that has committed to receive regular delivery of magazines, books, other goods, or services for a time period still in effect.

Address accuracy—The level of matches that a database attains when compared to a national address database. The accuracy of a mailing list (over 10,000 records) is required to be at least 95% accurate to qualify for best postal rates.

Address correction—The process of correcting addresses to match a national address database. This step is taken when a list does meet the 95% criteria (most lists require correction).

Address correction requested—An endorsement that authorizes CPC a fee to provide the new address, when known, of a person no longer at the address on the mailing piece.

ASCII (American Standard Code for Information Interchange)—A standard eight-bit data configuration in which seven bits are used to store data characters and, typically, the eighth bit is a parity bit.

Assigned mailing date(s)—The date(s) on which the list owner and the list user have agreed for the list user to mail a specific list.

Block—A specified quantity of logical records stored together between inter-record gaps, constituting a physical record.

Blocking factor—A statement of the number of logical records combined into one physical record or block on a storage medium, usually magnetic tape, between inter-record gaps.

BPI (bytes per inch)—The number of characters stored in an inch of magnetic tape. Commonly used densities are 800, 1,600, and 6,250.

Bulk mail center (BMC)—A large U.S. postal facility (currently there are 29 of them) that process and distribute mail to various SCFs.

Business list—Any list of individuals or companies based upon a business-associated interest, inquiry, membership, subscription, or purchase.

Buyer—One who has bought merchandise, books, records, information, or services. Unless another modifying word or two is used, it is assumed that a buyer has paid for all merchandise to date.

Buzzing—The process by which a computer program continuously selects various components within a name and address, and compares them to similar components in another record, thereby checking thousands of possibilities to locate a duplicate.

Carrier route presort (USPS)—The U.S. equivalent of a *letter carrier presort* in Canada. Mail that identifies the carrier route number for mail delivery. Mailers who sort down to carrier route can mail at a carrier route discount rate.

Cartridge (data cartridge)—A commonly used, transportable storage device for data coming from different computer systems. Cartridges are available in many *incompatible* shapes and sizes.

Cash buyer—A buyer who encloses payment with the order.

Catalogue request (paid/unpaid)—A person who sends for a catalogue, often a prospective buyer. The catalogue may be free, have a nominal charge for postage and handling, or available only at a substantial cost.

Cathode-ray tube display (CRT display)—(1) A device that presents data in a visual form by means of controlled electron beams. (2) The data display produced by the device as in (1).

Charge buyer—One who has ordered a product or service and paid for it after receipt of the product or service.

Cheshire label—Specially prepared paper on which names and addresses are printed before being mechanically affixed to a mailing piece, one at a time with permanent glue.

Cluster selection—A selection routine based upon taking a group of names in series, skipping a group, taking another group, etc. For example, a cluster selection on an Nth name basis might be the first 10 out of every 100 or the first 125 out of 175, etc.; a cluster selection using limited postal code might be the first 200 names in each of the specified postal codes, etc.

CMA Do Not Contact Service—A service provided by the Canadian Marketing Association that enables individuals to have their names and addresses removed from mailing, tele-marketing, or fax solicitation lists. Each is independent of the other, and Canadians may register for one or a combination of the services. These names are made available to both members and nonmembers of the association.

Compiled list—Names and addresses derived from direct-ories, newspapers, public records, trade show registrations, etc., that identify groups of people via a common link.

Consumer list—A list of names (usually at-home address) of people who have purchased merchandise, subscriptions, services, etc., from mail, Internet, radio, or TV solicitations.

Conversion—See *reformatting*.

Cross section—A group of names and addresses selected from a mailing list in such a way as to be representative of the entire list.

Database (list)—A number of lists, presumably with common interest, merged into one master list with duplicates eliminated.

Date control character (DCC)—The code applied to a pre-sorted record that denotes the period of time for which a sortation is valid. As the configuration of ZIP and postal codes change on a regular basis, each postal database is refreshed frequently, which ensures that each mail piece bears current information and can be delivered accurately.

Decoy—See *salting and seed*.

Demographics—Socioeconomic characteristics pertaining to a geographic unit (county, city, postal code, group of households, etc.).

Density (storage density)—A measure of the number of characters stored in a specified amount of space. For example, the number of characters per inch of magnetic tape (bytes per inch.)

Disk (magnetic diskette, floppy diskette)—A commonly used, transportable storage device for small amounts of data coming from a PC.

Distribution Centre Facility (DCF)—Level three within the National Presortation Schematic for CPC.

Donor list—A list of people and organizations that have given money to one or more charitable organizations.

Dump—Printed display of the contents of a data file, typically a magnetic tape or a portion of that data file, for purposes of review of the data.

Duplicate (dupe)—Two or more name and address records that are found to be equal under the list user's basis of comparison (match code, mathematical formula, etc.). Essentially, it is a record that matches another record. There are different kinds of duplicates. Personal dupes are the same person at the same address. Household dupes are different people at the same address.

Duplicate elimination—See *merge/purge*.

EBCDC (Extended Binary Coded Decimal Interchange Code)—This is an eight-bit configuration used to represent up to 256 separate characters (alpha, numeric, and special characters). EBCDIC uses the eighth bit as an information bit, which differs from ASCII, which uses one of the eight for parity.

Editing rules—Specific rules used in preparing name and address records in order to treat all elements the same way at all times. Although most companies use some editing rules in common, few conform in all respects. Therefore, knowledge of specific editing rules for each list is important to the user.

Escalation—The number of names ordered after a test. (See also *pyramiding*.)

Expire—A subscriber who has let a subscription run out without renewing it.

Field—A segment of a record that contains specific information. In a database, fields should contain the same information for each record. For example, all name fields should contain a name, all postal code fields should contain a postal code, etc.

Fielding—Technique by which the name and address of a record are divided into specific components.

File—A collection of records on a single storage device.

File layout—A way of laying out or formatting list information in a computer file that puts every piece of data in a specific position relative to every other piece of data and limits the amount of space assigned to that data. If any data is missing from an individual record or if its assigned space is not used completely, that space is not filled. Every record has the same space and the same length. Any data exceeding its assigned space limitation must be abbreviated, contracted, or truncated. (See also *record layout.*)

Forward Consolidation Point (FCP)—Level 4 within the National Presortation Schematic for CPC.

Forward Sortation Area (FSA)—The three-character code indicating a Canada Post Corporation distribution area. It is the first three characters of the six-character postal code. In urban areas, it describes an area roughly the size of 25 letter carrier routes.

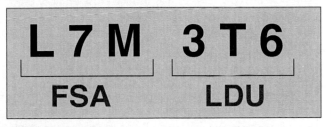

Free-standing insert—A promotional piece loosely inserted or nested in a newspaper or magazine.

Frequency—The number of times an individual has ordered within a specific period of time. (See also *recency.*)

House list (house file)—Any list of names owned by a company as a result of inquiry, buyer action, or specific targeting (usually with research).

Inter-list duplicate—Duplication of name and address records between two or more lists.

Intra-list duplicate—Duplication of name and address records within a given list.

Key code—Numbers or letters appended to a record that appear on a label, letter, reply, etc., which indicate a source of that name or segmentation for a mailing. This data is used for tracking and evaluation purposes.

Letter carrier presort (LCP)—Sequencing Canadian addresses by postal walk in order to obtain the highest possible postal discount when mailing third class.

Letter mail—CPC term for first-class mail.

Lettershop—A manufacturing facility (internal or external) that prepares mail for delivery to Canada Post Corporation (CPC).

List broker—A specialist who makes all necessary arrangements for one company to use the list(s) of other company(s). A broker's services may include most or all of the following: research, selection, recommendation, and subsequent evaluation.

List cleaning—The process of correcting and/or removing a name and address from a mailing list because it is no longer correct. Addresses may be corrected as a result of information furnished by the Postal Service or the individual. (See also *address correction requested.*) Removal may be the result of the return of a mailing piece by the Postal Service. (See also *return postage guaranteed.*)

Local delivery unit (LDU)—The last three characters of a Canadian postal code that denote a very small and easily defined section within an area described by the FSA. These characters can specify one side of a city block, an apartment building, an office building, or a large firm or organization that does considerable business with CPC. They can also denote a service from a post office or postal station.

Magnetic tape (mag tape)—A storage device for electronically recording and reproducing defined bits of data.

Merge—To combine multiple lists into a single list, all of which have the same file layout.

Merge/purge (duplicate elimination)—Combining two or more lists on a computer for the purpose of eliminating duplicate names and identifying multiple-buyers among the lists being used. Reports are then issued indicating, by list, the number of unique names, inter-file duplicates, assigned multi-buyers, and other pertinent information.

Net name arrangement—An agreement between list owner and list user in which the list owner agrees to accept adjusted payment for less than the total names shipped. Such arrangements can be for a percentage of names shipped or names actually mailed (whichever is greater), or for only those names actually mailed (without a percentage limitation). They can provide for a running charge or not. (See *running charge*.)

Nine-digit ZIP code (ZIP+4)—Within the United States, this provides for encoding each block face, each post office box, and each volume mail recipient with a unique nine-digit number.

Nixie—A mailing piece returned to a mailer (under proper authorization) by the Postal Service because of an incorrect or undeliverable name and address.

Nth name selection—A fractional unit that is repeated in sampling mailing list. For example, in an "every tenth" sample, you would select the 1st, 11th, 21st, 31st, etc. records or the 2nd, 12th, 22nd, 32nd, etc. records. Fractional Nths can also be processed.

Output—(1) The final results after a computer has processed data. (2) Information that has been transferred from the internal storage of a computer to external storage. (3) The process of transferring data from Internal to external storage—e.g., mag tape, hard copy printout, diskette, inkjet, etc. The client should always provide a document or sample of the mail piece indicating which fields in a given record are to be used when personalizing the mail piece.

Overlay—The process by which information is added to a main or master file to enable a more specialized selection.

Packed decimal—A means of data representation in which two numeric digits may be stored in a single eight-bit byte, thus increasing processing speed and storage capacity while minimizing record length in circumstances where neither alphabetic nor special characters need to be used.

Patterning—Technique that uses a series of words, word types, addresses, and address types to segment, standardize, and identify similarities and differences in the names and addresses of a file.

Penetration—Relationship of the number of individuals or families on a particular list (in total, by province, postal code, SIC code, etc.), compared to the total reachable population in the same area.

Point scoring—A flexible parameter set to determine the level in which a "possible duplicate" is identified as a "definite duplicate."

Postal code—A group of six characters used by Canada Post Corporation to designate specific post offices, stations, branches, buildings, or large companies. In urban areas, the LDU in conjunction with the FSA contain enough information to determine the destination of a letter right down to one side of a city street between intersections, and sometimes even further.

Pressure-sensitive label—A label that can be removed from its backing and reaffixed to another surface, such as an order form.

Printout—A hard copy display of information or data.

Psychographics—Characteristics or qualities used to denote the lifestyle(s) or attitude(s) of customers or prospective customers.

Purge—To remove records from a list, typically duplicate records.

Pyramiding—A method of testing mailing lists, starting with a small quantity and, based on positive indications, following with larger and larger quantities of the balance of the list until the entire list is finally mailed.

Recency—The latest purchase or other activity recorded for an individual or company on a specific customer list. (See also *frequency*.)

Record—A collection of related data or words treated as one unit.

Record layout—A written, field-by-field description of the data contained in a record, typically describing each field as to its length, beginning and ending positions, name, editing characteristics and data format (i.e., character, hex packed, etc.). (See also *file layout*.)

Reformatting—Changing a magnetic tape format from one arrangement to another more usable one. Also referred to as list or tape conversion.

Rented list—Lists that are rented by the organization performing the mailing.

Return date—The date specified on a list rental order on which the material is required by the mailers so that the mailing can get out on time.

Return postage guaranteed—An endorsement printed on the address face of envelopes or other mailing pieces if the mailer wishes the Postal Service to return undeliverable addressed admail. A charge will be made for each piece returned (see also *list cleaning*).

Running charge—The price charged by a list owner for names run or passed, but not used, by a specific mailer. When such a charge is made, it usually covers extra processing costs. However, some list owners set the price without regard to actual cost.

Salting—Deliberate placing of decoy or dummy names in a list to trace list usage and delivery. (See also *decoy and seed.*)

Sample package (mailing piece)—An example of the package to be mailed by the list user to a particular list. Such a mailing piece is submitted to the list owner for approval prior to commitment for one-time use of that list. Although a sample package may, due to time pressure, differ slightly from the actual package used, the list user agreement usually requires the user to reveal any material differences when submitting the sample package.

Scratch—The process by which a physical reel of magnetic tape that contains a data file is made available for reuse when there is no longer any need to retain the data file. In general, this process involves obtaining authorization (from the responsible account service person) to scratch, removing physical external labels from the reel, placing a write ring in the physical reel, and updating tape library records.

Seed—A name especially inserted into a mailing list for verification of list usage. It has unique characteristics, such as an order number or a unique spelling, that indicates order for which it was used. (See also *decoy and salting.*)

Select—To choose a group of records from a database based on a given criteria.

SIC (Standard Industrial Classification)—Classification of business, as defined by the Canadian and U.S. governments.

Sort—A processing function that arranges a file in a specified sequence.

Source code—Unique alphabetical and/or numeric identification for distinguishing one list or media source from another. (See also *key code*.)

Split test—Two or more samples from the same list, selected by the same criteria (such as an A/B split) used for testing different packages, offers, mail dates, or any other part of the mailing.

Suppress (suppression)—To eliminate certain records based on a given criteria.

Tape density—The number of bits of information that can be included in each inch of a specific magnetic tape (e.g., 556, 800, or 1,600).

Tape dump—A printout of data on a magnetic tape for checking correctness, readability, consistency, etc.

Tape layout—A written, field-by-field description of the data contained in a record, typically describing each field as to its length, beginning and ending positions, name, editing characteristics, and data format (i.e., character, hex, packed, etc.).

Test panel—A term used to identify each of the parts or samples in a split test.

Title—A designation before (prefix) or after (suffix) a name that more accurately identifies an individual. Prefixes include Mr., Mrs., Ms., Dr., Sister, etc. Suffixes include MD, Jr., PhD, President, Sales Manager, etc.

Truncate—To drop characters at the end of a data field because the field being converted or keyed in is too long to fit in the record position in which it must be stored.

Universe count—The total number on a list available within a particular selection, taking no account of prior usage.

Update—Adding recent transactions and current information to the master (main) list to reflect the current status of each record on the list.

Upper/lower conversion—Converting a database, commonly all in capital letters, to uppercase and lowercase letters. (Note: Upper/lower conversion is not 100% accurate. For example, some names such as MacArthur may result in Macarthur.)

Variable field—A way of laying out or formatting list information that assigns a specific sequence to the data, but does not assign it specific positions. While this method conserves space on magnetic tape and adds flexibility for the end user, it generally is a more difficult format for programmers.

Glossary 2—Lettershop Terms

Bindery—Conversion of printed sheet into finished product.

Cheshire label—An address label that is approximately 1 in. (25 mm) deep and 3 in. (76 mm) wide. Often used for catalogues and books. For example, *TV Guide* uses Cheshire labels.

Closed leading edge—The leading edge of a piece going into an envelope should be folded.

Digitize—A logo, signature, or any graphic that can be digitized and then laser-imaged onto a page. This allows for different signatures or logos to be used in the same mailing yet retain the density of the mailing to receive maximum postal discounts.

Friction feeder—An add-on piece of equipment used to facilitate the insertion of a piece with an open leading edge, such as an accordion-folded piece.

Indicia (permit)—The preprinted block in the upper right-hand corner of an address area, which signifies that a mailing has been paid for. Permits are available for standard, first, and catalogue classes.

Inkjet imaging—A manner of addressing a mail piece (self-mailer, envelope, catalogue, etc.). The address area of the mail piece is run under a head that sprays fine "jets" of ink to generate an address. Inkjet imaging is usually used to personalize addresses and possibly account numbers.

Laser—A means of personalizing an entire page of information. Typically used for more involved personalization and letter type direct mail for a slicker look. More personalized look equates to a higher cost. Used quite often for financial and high-end promotion.

Laser, continuous—Laser imaging that is performed in a continuous format, either fan-folded or on rolls. Typically used for larger runs since setup costs are high.

Laser, cut-sheet—Laser imaging that is performed on single sheets. Sheet sizes can be from $8\frac{1}{2}\times11$ in. (216×279 mm) to 14×17 in. (356×432 mm). Odd sizes and grain direction should be discussed prior to quoting.

Mail preparation (sort, bag, and bundle)—The process of preparing mail in order to obtain second- or third-class postage rates.

Meter—A means of affixing postage to an envelope. Meters are set to affix a certain amount of postage to an envelope and can be used for first class, standard mail, and parcels. Meter money is required prior to mail production.

Oversize—A term for standard mail pieces that have dimensions exceeding standard sizes. Oversize pieces involve higher postal costs and usually cost more to produce.

INDEX

A

B

C

S

T

U

V

W

X

About the Authors

T.J. Tedesco is the founder and president of Grow Sales, Inc., a consulting company exclusively serving the promotional needs of the direct mail and graphic arts industries since 1996. Tedesco and the Grow Sales team help companies of all sizes achieve their business objectives by winning top-of-mind positioning. Grow Sales, Inc. offers the following: marketing management, public relations, web and graphic design, sales support, and business advisory services.

Tedesco has a BA in English from Grinnell College and an MBA in Marketing and Finance from Northeastern University, where he was class valedictorian. He is a well-known speaker in the direct mail and graphic arts industries and is a regular columnist for *High Volume Printing*. He has authored *Binding, Finishing & Mailing: The Final Word, 1st ed.* (1999), *Win Top-of-Mind Positioning* (2000), *Direct Mail Pal* (2002), and *Binding, Finishing & Mailing: The Final Word, 2nd ed.* (2005). In addition, he has published hundreds of articles in dozens of other industry-related publications.

Prior to launching his consulting business, Tedesco was the director of marketing for a large graphic arts company and a product manager for a consumer products company. He also has sold graphic arts machinery, printing, and binding services. He started his career in finance with a Fortune 100 company.

Tedesco lives Rockville, Maryland, where he still plays both baseball and hockey.

He can be reached at 301-294-9900 or tj@growsales.com.
His company's website is www.growsales.com.

John Leonard is vice president, sales and marketing for SMART DM (formerly SMR•Tytrek), located in Toronto, Canada. Leonard has a degree in general advertising and started his career with a direct marketing company owned by Grey Advertising. When this company was sold to SMR, he shifted his attention to sales and customer service.

In 1997 SMR merged with the oldest specialty finishing organization in Canada, Tytrek Graphic Finishers. Today, SMART DM is one of Canada's premier specialty mailing services companies, offering a diverse array of binding, finishing, and mailing services allowing for direct mail programs that range from standard #10 packages to highly complex variably imaged self-mailers.

As a firm believer in the power of direct mail, Leonard passes on his knowledge by providing direct mail production seminars for the CMA, speaks regularly for the direct marketing certification course, has taught part-time at Mohawk College, sits on the Advertising Advisory Board for Mohawk, and has contributed to one other direct mail book and co-authored the first *Direct Mail Pal.*

He can be reached at 416-461-9271 or
jleonard@smartdm.ca

David Engel was born and raised in Montreal. He attended McGill University where he graduated with a degree in commerce, specializing in marketing. Engel went on to do graduate work at the Rochester Institute of Technology before joining his father's company, Metro-Graphics, in sales and marketing.

As founder and president of Innovative Graphics, a specialty printing and marketing services company since 1995, Engel has earned a reputation as an innovator in the direct marketing industry. His organization partners with clients to solve creative challenges and increase response rates by matching their needs with state-of-the-art production technologies.

Engel is also an active member of the Executive Committee and Board of Directors of the Canadian Marketing Association (CMA), and the incoming chair of the board of the United Jewish Appeal/Jewish Federation of Greater Toronto.

He can be reached at 416-410-0576 or
dengel@innovativegraphics.com

About PIA/GATF

The Printing Industries of America, Inc./Graphic Arts Technical Foundation (PIA/GATF), along with its affiliates, deliver products and services that enhance the growth, efficiency, and profitability of its members and the industry through advocacy, education, research, and technical information.

The 1999 consolidation of PIA and GATF brought together two powerful partners: the world's largest graphic arts trade association representing an industry with more than 1 million employees and $156 billion in sales and a nonprofit, technical, scientific, and educational organization dedicated to the advancement of the graphic communications industries worldwide.

Founded in 1924, the Foundation's staff of researchers, educators, and technical specialists help members in more than 80 countries maintain their competitive edge by increasing productivity, print quality, process control, and environmental compliance and by implementing new techniques and technologies. Through conferences, Internet symposia, workshops, consulting, technical support, laboratory services, and publications, PIA/GATF strives to advance a global graphic communications community.

In continuous operation since 1887, PIA promotes programs, services, and an environment that helps its members operate profitably. Many of PIA's members are commercial printers, allied graphic arts firms such as electronic imaging companies, equipment manufacturers, and suppliers. To serve the unique needs of specific segments of the print and graphic communications industries, PIA developed special industry groups, sections, and councils. Each provides members with current information on their specific segment, helping them to meet the business challenges of a constantly changing environment. Special industry groups include the Web Offset Association

(WOA), Label Printing Industries of America (LPIA), and Binding Industries Association (BIA). The sections include Printing Industry Financial Executives (PIFE), Sales & Marketing Executives (S&ME), Digital Printing Council (DPC), and the E-Business Council (EBC).

PIA/GATFPress publishes books on nearly every aspect of the field; training curricula; audiovisuals (CD-ROMs and videocassettes); and research and technology reports. It also publishes GATFWorld, a bimonthly magazine providing articles on industry technologies, trends, and practices, and Management Portfolio, a bimonthly magazine that provides information on business management practices for printers; economic trends, benchmarks, and forecasts; legislative and regulatory affairs; human and industrial relations issues; sales, marketing, and customer service techniques; and management resources.

For more information about PIA/GATF, special industry groups, sections, products, and services, visit www.gain.net.

PIA/GATF*Press:* Selected Titles

The Basics of Print Production. Hardesty, Mary

Binding, Finishing, and Mailing: The Final Word. Tedesco, T.J.

Customer Service in the Printing Industry. Colbary, Richard E.

Direct Mail Pal. Tedesco, T.J., Ken Boone, Terry Woods, & John Leonard

Encyclopedia of Graphic Communications. Romano, Frank J. & Richard M. Romano

Flexography Primer. Crouch, J. Page

Gravure Primer. Kasunich, Cheryl L.

Guide to Desktop Publishing. Hinderliter, Hal

Handbook of Graphic Arts Equations. Breede, Manfred

Lithography Primer. Wilson, Daniel G.

Nine Steps to Effective and Efficient Color Press OKs for Offset Printing. Biegert, Diane J.

On-Demand and Digital Printing Primer. Fenton, Howard M.

Paper Buying Primer. Wilson, Lawrence A.

Printscape: A Crash Course in Graphic Communications. Wilson, Daniel G., Deanna M. Gentile, and PIA/GATF Staff

Real-Time Marketing: New Rules for the New Media. Morris-Lee, James

Screen Printing Primer. Ingram, Samuel T.

Understanding Graphic Communication: Selected Readings. Levenson, Harvey Robert.

The Very Last Designer's Guide to Digital, On-Demand, and Variable-Data Color Printing. Clark, David & Frank J. Romano

Win Top-of-Mind Positioning: Graphic Arts Sales & Marketing Excellence. Tedesco, T.J., Mike Stevens, & Henry Mortimer

Colophon

Direct Mail Pal—Canada was edited, designed, and printed at PIA/GATF, headquartered in Sewickley, Pennsylvania. The text was created by the authors using Microsoft Word, then edited at PIA/GATF, and finally imported into QuarkXPress on an Apple Power Macintosh. The primary fonts used for the interior of the book are Gill Sans and Eurostile Condensed. Page proofs for author approval were printed on a Xerox DC 470ST Document Centre, as well as output as Adobe Acrobat PDF files.

Once the editorial/page layout process was completed, the images were transmitted to PIA/GATF's Robert Howard Center for Imaging Excellence, where all images were adjusted for the printing parameters of PIA/GATF's in-house printing department and proofed.

Adobe PDF files were made from the QuarkXPress files and then transmitted by internal network to PIA/GATF's on-demand printing department. The interior and cover of the book were both printed on a Xerox iGen3 Digital Production Press. Finally, the book was bound inline using the Bourg Book Factory.